B WLING

HOW TO MASTER THE GAME
BY PARKER BOHN III
WITH THE BRUNSWICK PRO STAFF

BY PARKER BOHN III
WITH THE BRUNSWICK PRO STAFF
WRITTEN WITH DAN HERBST

BOW

HOW TO MAS

FOREWORD BY JOHNNY PETRAGLIA
INTRODUCTION BY DREW CAREY

LING

TER THE GAME

PRINCIPAL PHOTOGRAPHY BY
SIMON BRUTY AND JOHN MUTRUX

Brunswick UNIVERSE PUBLISHING

DESIGN AND ILLUSTRATION: OPTO DESIGN

FIRST PUBLISHED IN THE UNITED STATES OF AMERICA IN 2000
BY UNIVERSE PUBLISHING
A DIVISION OF RIZZOLI INTERNATIONAL PUBLICATIONS, INC.
300 PARK AVENUE SOUTH
NEW YORK, NY 10010

In every sport there are certain athletes whose attributes are so pronounced that the first time you see them you know they are destined for greatness. That was my first impression when I initially competed against Parker Bohn III in 1985. I wasn't wrong. Nor was I alone. ABC-TV commentator Nelson Burton Jr. pegged Parker for stardom during Parker's first television appearance. I can recall that evening when Parker told me that he was surprised that he was receiving so much praise; at that time he had probably earned only about twenty thousand dollars in competitions.

Possessing fantastic technique, the ideal build for a bowler, great determination, and a superior mental game, Parker became the preeminent left-handed player of the nineties. He capped the decade by becoming the last Bowler of the Year of the twentieth century. Parker didn't merely claim 1999 top performer recognition, he finished one of the most impressive years in the PBA's history. Well into the fall tour he had more than doubled the official earnings of his nearest rival, an unprecedented feat. He ended the year lead-ing the tour in points, earnings, wins (his five titles more than doubling the two won by the next nearest player), and championship round appearances (eleven in twenty-four events). For good measure, his yearly average shattered Walter Ray Williams's previous PBA record by nearly two full pins.

During the 1990s Parker won twenty events on the PBA's national tour. To put that into perspective, consider that as of the century's end only eight other players had captured more tournaments—during their entire careers. At the time I'm writing this, he seems well on course to join legends Earl Anthony, Mark Roth, and Walter Ray Williams in the thirty-win club. Parker remains a solid candidate to eclipse Earl's record of forty-one career triumphs. I am convinced that when Parker's great career finally comes to an end that he will have a good chance of being considered one of the five candidates for the best of all time.

His eight straight years of bagging official earnings of more than $100,000 during an era of shrinking prize funds is an enviable model of consistency. The only superstars who are even close to him in this category are Walter Ray and Marshall Holman, who both finished six straight years of earning this much. Mark Roth is next at five years.

As popular with fans as he is respected by his peers, Parker became the first player in PBA history to have his own fan club. That the Bohn Zone currently boasts members from every inhabited continent owes, in part, to Parker's friendliness, accessibility to spectators, and his having been the only player to have captured back-to-back Japan Cups. He's also a four-time winner of the Steve Nagy Sportsmanship Award that is annually presented to the man whose fellow pros deem to have demonstrated the finest standards of comportment. In short, he's a class act.

His extraordinary feats aside, I can think of no bowler who would be better qualified to write this instructional book. I know it's something of a cliché, but it's absolutely true that he is a consummate student of the game.

To watch Parker in action is to observe a style unsurpassed in bowling. His timing, armswing, follow-through, and footwork are all superb. He possesses a wide range of effective hand releases and is among the best in the business at modifying his ball speed to conquer any variety of lane condition. All of these attributes are possible only if one truly understands the components of a sport. The fact that Parker has such an understanding—as well as an ability to break down these components for others—will become evident as you read what follows.

I know that all players—from the most highly ambitious to the once-a-week league participant—will greatly benefit from the information that Parker will present to you. His thoroughness and professionalism will serve to help you fulfill your potential on the lanes and, with that, your enjoyment of this great sport.

—Johnny Petraglia

If you're reading this in the bookstore wondering if you need a book on bowling or not, then yeah, you probably do. Nobody thinks about buying a bowling book if they're already good at it.

Now, if you were like me, you wouldn't need this book. I'm already good. How good? I once bowled a 250. Since you're obviously new to the game, trust me when I tell you that 250 is a very, very good score. It's the kind of score that makes women weak in the knees. I know. I've seen it.

I don't need Parker Bohn telling me what a good approach is, and how to do a proper release. I've got that down. 250 baby. You don't get a score like that without a good release.

My average? Well, not to brag, but it's in the low-to-mid hundred-something range. That's hundred, as in lots. Like I said, I'm beyond books. And I've got the style, baby—the shoes, the shirts, the cool-looking bag. I mean, I'm telling you, I scare people when I stroll into the Family Fun Center. Who needs a book when you can beat people with your style? Not me, man.

I wish I was writing a bowling book. I could give you some advice you could use. Here, check this out:

1.

Bowling balls weigh a ton. You can't believe the effort it takes just to get them in and out of the trunk of your car. Jeez-oh-man, they're a pain. But! You should never put them in a bag with wheels on it. Never! It shows weakness and will all but ensure your defeat if anyone sees you "rolling your balls in."

2.

Bowling pins have stickum on the bottoms of them. Especially the 7 and 10 pins. Honest. The PBA and the American Bowling Congress don't want you to know this, but I'm not afraid to tell you the truth. Anyway, what can you do about it? Nothing. Just realize that every time you leave a corner pin, The Man is out to get you.

3.

The more bowling gloves and resin bags and other miscellaneous bowling junk you buy, the better you'll bowl.

Now that's righteous knowledge, brother. Not this "how to make a spare" crap. I would give you stuff that you could use. Oh well. This is Parker's book, not mine.

Speaking of Parker Bohn, let me tell you a little story about this guy, the guy you're about to indirectly give your money to by buying his book: Once, after a big tournament in Ohio (I wasn't in it—the PBA banned me for exposing their little "bowling pin stickum" scam), Parker and I decided to go out and raise some heck like the righteous bowling cats that we are.

Long story short, we end up at my brother Roger's house watching *South Park* , the movie, on cable, and Parker is rolling his eyes at all the dirty words. Can you believe it? And you want to learn bowling from him? Just because he rolls a perfect game every once in a while and he's won a bunch of tournaments? Good luck.

Well, I won't keep you. You probably want to wander over to the "What's New in Paperback" section while you're here and pick up a few things. And, hey—don't worry about your game. You'll read this book, practice . . . it'll get better. And then who knows? Maybe someday you'll get a "250" ring just like mine.

—Drew Carey
"Mr. 250"

PREFACE: BOWLING'S LONG LEGACY

The origins of bowling are known to date back several millennia, with many forms of the game having since emerged all around the globe. However, the exact details of its evolution are, to put it mildly, sketchy. Ample evidence demonstrates that bowling in some form or other dates back about four thousand years to Rome and Greece, and some clues suggest it may have been played even earlier. In the 1930s an archeologist named Sir Flinders Petrie discovered what was believed to be a seven-thousand-year-old tomb of an Egyptian child. In it he found implements somewhat similar to those he was familiar with from the sport of skittles as it was being played in his native Norfolk, England. Among the items discovered were a stone ball and nine conical pieces of stone that are thought to have served as an early form of pins. Those findings certainly give new meaning to those of us who bemoan "burying the 10-pin"!

Attributing bowling's introduction to prehistoric Egypt says nothing of the great contributions of two of the sport's most important role models, Barney Rubble and Fred Flintstone. We certainly have plenty of evidence, including documents of the action from Bedrock Bowl.

Some slightly more substantial evidence tells us that two thousand years ago people played a game in the Italian Alps that involved the tossing of stone objects in order to land closer to other stone objects. Supposedly this game became popular among Roman soldiers, who then spread it throughout the empire. This led to the outdoor bowling game now known as boccie, as well as the game of bowls.

Very little artifacts remain for us to connect these early roots to the game's marked presence in Europe at the end of the medieval age. According to bowling historian Bruce Pluckhahn, the use of modern pins most likely began as part of a religious ceremony in Germany. In *The Encyclopedia of Sports*, he notes: "As early as the third and fourth century A.D., strange rites often would be held in the cloisters of churches. The parishioner would be told to place his ever-present kegel—the implement most Germans carried for sports and self-protection—at one end of a runway resembling today's bowling lane. A stone was rolled at the [kegel], those successfully toppling it having cleansed themselves of sin." In the early 1500s Martin Luther was one priest who especially enjoyed his kegels. Though he went on to denounce the church, he always had bowling as a pastime to relieve the stress of protesting so much. He built several alleys so he and his children could play at home.

Bowling became quite popular in Britain in the early days as well. So popular in fact, that King Edward III outlawed the game in 1366 because his soldiers were skipping their archery practice to play at bowls. The sport persisted and grew despite this. According to an old tale, in 1588 when the English admiral Sir Francis Drake was told in midgame that the Spanish Armada was about to attack the English fleet, he calculated that he had sufficient time to conquer his lane opponent before joining his troops to defeat the Spaniards. Luckily for England, he was right. In these early days, bowling was almost always played outdoors, with the lanes consisting of hard-packed mud or wooden planks. Eventually the game was brought indoors, probably first in England in the 1400s.

Europeans from all different countries brought along their forms of bowling with them to the New World. Supposedly when Sir Thomas Dale came to rescue the failing settlement of Jamestown, Virginia, in 1611, he found the surviving colonists engaged in a match of bowls. The Dutch settlers of New Amsterdam (now better known as New York) played the game extensively in the 1600s. Overlooking the vast battery at the southern tip of Manhattan, they would gather for lawn play. (That section of New York City is still known as Bowling Green but has now given its name to a subway station.) During colonial times, the sport, then played with nine pins, was banned in several domains to combat the drinking and gambling that consistently accompanied the competition.

These shady associations with the game continued into the nineteenth century. In 1820 Washington Irving published his classic tale of a henpecked husband, Rip Van Winkle, whose notorious twenty-year sleep was rudely interrupted by "long, rolling-peals, like distant thunder." Upon awakening, he soon learned that the noises were those made by "a company of odd-looking personages playing at nine-pins." New York City saw some of the first indoor lanes built in 1840, at Knickerbocker Alleys. More and more indoor centers followed this one, attracting more and more gamblers. Then laws were enacted to outlaw nine-pins. No problem. Legend has it that a clever and anonymous soul merely added a pin and called the "new" game bowling.

The addition of the new pin and the building of indoor lanes both brought about a huge period of expansion in the game. It was now separated from its darker past of gambling and drinking and became more of a wholesome, clean sport with appeal for men and women of all classes. By the middle of the

THE DUTCH SETTLERS OF NEW AMSTERDAM
(NOW KNOWN AS NEW YORK CITY)
WERE AMONG THE FIRST TO BRING BOWLING
TO AMERICA.

THE END OF THE NINE-
TEENTH CENTURY SAW
MANY ATTEMPTS TO
ORGANIZE THE SPORT.
IT WASN'T UNTIL THE
AMERICAN BOWLING
CONGRESS (ABC)
WAS FOUNDED IN
1895 THAT COMMON
STANDARDS WERE
ADOPTED ACROSS
THE NATION. SOON
AFTER, IN 1901,
THE FIRST ABC TOUR-
NAMENT WAS HELD
IN CHICAGO.

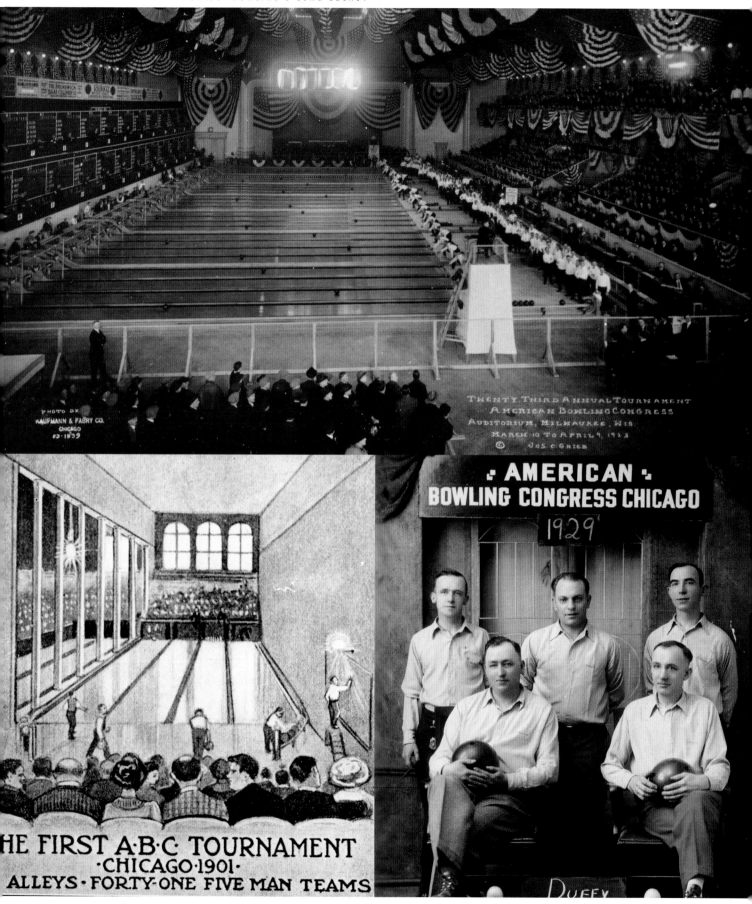

PHOTO BY
KAUFMANN & FABRY CO.
CHICAGO
82-1929

TWENTY THIRD ANNUAL TOURNAMENT
AMERICAN BOWLING CONGRESS
AUDITORIUM, MILWAUKEE, WIS
MARCH 10 TO APRIL 4, 1923
© JOS. C GRIEB

AMERICAN
BOWLING CONGRESS CHICAGO
1929

DUFFY

HE FIRST A·B·C· TOURNAMENT
·CHICAGO·1901·
ALLEYS · FORTY·ONE FIVE MAN TEAMS

nineteenth century indoor lanes were spreading westward across the land and became seen as the essential American sport. President Abraham Lincoln became a great fan of the game, as did Mark Twain. Rich industrialists built private lanes in their mansions, and the wives of tycoons John Astor and Cornelius Vanderbilt were among the regular upscale clients at Knickerbocker Alleys in New York, which had become a mecca of bowling. German immigrants helped to strengthen the sport's hold, and toward the end of the 1800s approximately two hundred alleys were in existence in New York City alone. But, as with snowflakes, it often seemed as if no two bowling establishments were alike.

EMERGENCE OF THE MODERN GAME

The push for standardization was inevitable in order for bowlers to compete in matches around the country. Other sports, such as basketball and baseball, were also at the same time in the throes of becoming organized. In 1875 nine bowling clubs sent twenty-seven representatives to Germania Hall in New York City. The resulting National Bowling Association had a limited local influence and an even more limited lifespan. Nevertheless, it enacted three major rules that remain today: the headpin was to be sixty feet from the foul line, fallen pins were to be removed from the alley before any subsequent shot could be thrown, and any ball that fell into the channel was out of play. However, the NBA's mandated pin size didn't sit well with proprietors whose facilities would have had to change. Most simply ignored the edict. In 1890 the American Bowling League was formed. It reduced pin size to today's fifteen-inch height and changed frames from three shots to two. But, like the NBA, it had no enforcement powers, and chaos still ruled.

A letter to the editor published in the *New York Sun* in 1890 from a William Sielken of Brooklyn's Ivanhoe Bowling Club first put forth the idea of attaching a number to each of the ten pins. Mr.

Sielken was seeking a timely solution to the common problem of how to allow bowlers to call out immediately which of the pins hadn't been properly spotted by the pinboys, whose job it was to reset the pins after each frame. Academy Alleys was the first to number the spots where the pins were to be placed. The innovation, though it faced with initial resistance, eventually took hold.

There could be no doubting the commercial potential of bowling, but the sport needed an organizing force. For five years Moses Bensinger, who was a leader of the Brunswick company in the latter part of the 1800s, ceaselessly campaigned for the founding of a governing body, and he was not a lone voice in the wilderness. Another highly influential driving force for rules standardization was the United Bowling Clubs, with 120 member clubs, led by avid bowler Joe Thum.

Sporting a mile-wide white mustache and often a jacket decorated to the hilt with pins, he looked every bit the sea captain from central casting. Having immigrated to the United States as a teenager from Pfullendorf, Germany, just after the Civil War, Thum ran a Bavarian restaurant that was so popular that he had little time for his favorite activity. His solution was to construct two lanes in the restaurant's basement and, shortly thereafter, to add six lanes to Germania Hall.

Thum's tireless campaigning along with the efforts of others led to the launch of the American Bowling Congress at New York City's Beethoven Hall on September 9, 1895. It soon established rules and regulations that included the pin size and two-frame shots that the defunct NBA had previously set, as well as lane width and length. Thanks to the these common standards, it wasn't long before the game had grown significantly in popularity. With further prodding from Bensinger, the ABC held its first championship tournament in 1901. Forty-one teams converged on Chicago, lured, in part, by a prize fund of twelve hundred dollars. The new event was not without

BY 1900, NEW YORK CITY HAD ALMOST TWO HUNDRED BOWLING ALLEYS.

controversy. New York's John Voorhies's 633 series was apparently rolled with an oversized ball (the measuring ring would not fit over it). However, since no other balls were checked his score was allowed to stand. In turn, when the Windy City's Frank Brill edged out the Big Apple's John Koster for all-events honors, the New York delegation claimed that lanes five and six were superior to the others. They might have had a case, as all of the titles went to players who had competed

1916 an encore event saw forty of the best women players from around the country competing for a $222 total purse. The following year the players passed bylaws to form the Women's National Bowling Association. Their first official tournament was held in Cincinnati's Freeman Avenue Armory and it attracted thirty-two teams vying for $1,347.

As more and more played, everyday bowlers contributed their own advancements to the game. In the 1930s Sully

on that pair. Meanwhile, having shot 2,720, the hometown Standard Club walked off with the top prize of two hundred dollars in team play.

If New York was the early mecca of bowling, then St. Louis was surely the center of women's tenpins. Coinciding with the ABC tournaments in 1907 and 1911, St. Louis proprietor Dennis Sweeney held what were billed as "national" competitions for females. In

Bates, an engineer for Buick Motors, was bowling with a woman who was having trouble holding on to her ball. At that time balls were drilled so that only the thumb and middle finger were inserted. Bates reasoned that adding a hole for the ring finger and angling the thumb hole would solve her problem. Thus was the so-called Bates Grip introduced. It wasn't long before virtually every bowler was sold on the third hole.

ABOVE: JOE THUM (CENTER) WAS A GERMAN IMMIGRANT WHO RAN A NEW YORK CITY BOWLING ALLEY IN THE FIRST YEARS OF THE TWENTIETH CENTURY. HIS TIRELESS CAMPAIGNING LED TO THE ESTABLISHMENT OF THE ABC.

THE ENGLISH GAME OF BOWLS, WHICH RESEMBLES A BLEND OF BOWLING AND BOC-CIE, HAS REMAINED A POPULAR SPORT OVER THE AGES AND IS STILL PLAYED TODAY IN FORMAL LAWN TOURNAMENTS.

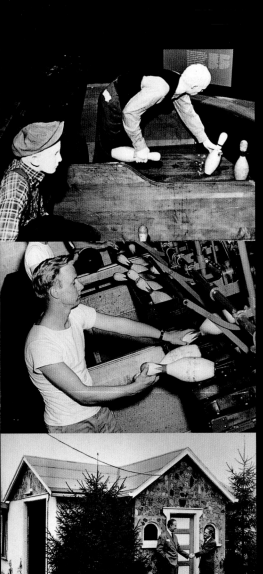

Many of our sport's all-time legendary stars, such as Joe Norris and Dick Weber, got their starts as pinboys. At the turn of the century, setting pins was a burdensome and often painful job (see re-created scene at left, top), but thanks to an innovation that was introduced in 1907, pinboys like Joe and Dick had it relatively easy. Known as the automatic pinsetter, the device allowed the pinboy to place the ten pins into holes in a triangular-shaped rack that was subsequently lowered by pulling a lever (seen at left, top center). This was no small step forward as it both decreased the amount of time required to restart the game and saved the shins of many a pinboy from the damage caused when an absent-minded bowler rolled a shot before the unfortunate laborer could jump out of the way.

Joe Norris remembers that those early pinsetters were aided by a tiny hole on the bottom of each pin that was lowered onto a small protruding spike. Upon releasing the lever, the spikes disappeared into the floor of the lane. Joe's initial rate in the 1920s was a nickel a game. Although Joe was on the up-and-up, many of his fellow pinboys happily swapped their integrity for greater compensation. There is no telling just how many high-stakes games in smoke-filled alleys were influenced by a pinboy on the take who nudged over an occasional pin to make certain that his secret benefactor could convert an easy spare rather than be confronted with a split. When competing, Joe Norris made it a point to station a friend behind the pin deck to make certain that when his opponent shot the laws of gravity weren't violated by a pinboy whose greased palm inspired soccerlike skills. "Some of those guys," Norris says with a chuckle, "were pretty clever with their feet."

Perhaps the most colorful incident of the pinboy era was the near riot over their presence in Pittsburgh during the 1909 ABC tournament. On the eve of the event the pinboys, many of whom had traveled great distances to work at bowling's premier event, staged a wildcat strike while demanding greater pay and shorter hours. The authorities responded in the typical fashion of the era by immediately bringing in scabs. Several pinboys refused to abandon their posts. With the tournament start delayed, those who insisted on holding their ground were forcibly removed.

Like many lane proprietors, George Beckerle was often frustrated at being at the mercy of pinboys, many of whom also lacked reliability and civility. Beckerle discussed his idea of a mechanical device to remove and setup pins with his customers, including three men who worked across the street at the Dexter Folding Company. Gottfried Schmidt, John McElroy, and Fred Sandhage spent years tinkering in the henhouse of Sandhage's turkey farm in Pearl River, New York (seen at left, bottom center), before Schmidt registered a patent on April 8, 1944, for an automatic pin-spotting apparatus.

A prototype was set up in a garage opposite the ABC tournament in upstate Buffalo in 1946. Initial performances were far from reassuring, and it took five years and $15 million worth of research for improvement until AMF installed the first commercially produced machines at the Bowl-O-Drome in Mount Clemens, Michigan (seen at left, bottom). By 1954, some 86 centers with 1,651 lanes had made pinboys every bit as extinct as dinosaurs. Two years later the figure had risen to 9,000 lanes.

Only a handful of centers today don't feature the automatic pinspotters. But if you're the sentimental sort, you can still wander into the basement of the St. Louis–based International Bowling Hall of Fame and Museum to experience what it's like to roll a game the old-fashioned way.

During the following decade, Connie Schwoegler was a talented player with a badly injured middle finger and small, arthritis-prone hands. He decided to try out an experiment in the hope of finding a remedy for his discomfort—he inserted his fingers only partially into his ball. Inadvertently, he discovered a grip that provided for a far more effective hooking action. Schwoegler won the All-Star in 1949. He was then retained by Brunswick to promote the innovative drilling approach. Thus was the fingertip grip launched and popularized. Also during that decade, serious players began having their balls custom drilled to fit their needs.

The innovation that truly revolutionized the game was the automatic pinspotter. Back in 1911 Brunswick had hired a Norwegian inventor named Ernest Hedenskoog with the mandate to make pinboys obsolete. However, after thirty years, the closest he came was a magnetic device that could pick up pins, which never caught on. Then in 1944 Gottfried Schmidt invented an apparatus that held much more promise. The American Machine and Foundry company (AMF), which had recently entered the bowling business, picked up on this invention and installed the first public machines in 1951. Soon the whole country was using automatic pinspotters and pinboys had to look for new work.

Automated equipment meant that bowlers were no longer dependent on pinboys; there was much less time wasted waiting for the pins to be racked. Facilities were able to expand, and participation soared. In less than twenty years the number of lanes across America nearly tripled. The boom was so substantial that for a time it seemed that it was mandatory for a baseball star to own his own facility. Among the sluggers with centers were Mickey Mantle, Gil Hodges, Stan Musial, Yogi Berra, Joe Garagiola, and Phil Rizzuto.

ONE COMPANY'S ROLE

Brunswick, launched in 1845 by Swiss immigrant John Brunswick, initially made billiard tables and cabinetry. In 1884 the need for diversification led to a move into the burgeoning bowling business over a decade before the ABC was founded. At the time balls were made out of lignum vitae (hardwood); rubber balls began appearing just after the start of the new century. Although the first of the rubber species was produced by New York's American Hard Rubber Company, the big splash came in 1914 when Brunswick introduced the Mineralite, touted as consisting of a "mysterious rubber compound." At twenty dollars it was far from economical by the standards of the era. Perhaps that's why of the many places that one could obtain the Mineralite several were jewelry stores. To ensure adequate attention to its first major bowling innovation, the company sent its ball on an around-the-world tour that included stops in front of some heads of state.

Brunswick introduced another feature that would help eliminate the human element from impeding upon a fair result. In 1939 in Los Angeles's Luxor Bowl the foul light, with its dreaded buzzer, made its debut. No longer would judges sitting atop elevated chairs have to determine whether the bowler's toe had broken the plane of the foul line.

That Brunswick was still around on the eve of U.S. involvement in the Second World War owed much to the great-grandson of the company's founder. Had it not been for the yeoman efforts of Robert F. Bensinger, what is now the oldest sporting goods company in the United States would never have survived the Depression. During the four-year period beginning in 1928, yearly sales dropped from $29.5 million to $3.9 million. Brunswick suffered annual seven-figure losses during the first half of the 1930s. Bensinger decided to sell the company's phonograph and

LEFT: IN 1914 BRUNSWICK LAUNCHED THE MINERALITE, ONE OF THE FIRST RUBBER BALLS. *ABOVE:* THE MINERALITE WENT ON A TOUR OF AMERICA AND EUROPE, EVEN MAKING STOPS BEFORE SEVERAL HEADS OF STATE.

recording business to Warner Brothers, thereby rescuing Brunswick.

Bensinger's postwar efforts toward more comfortable and visually appealing centers helped to entice women and families to bowl. The company's 1956 installation of its first automatic pinspotter in addition to Bensinger's decision to sign many of the top pros of his era for coast-to-coast exhibitions and personal appearances, helped to solidify bowling's subsequent participation boom. The early staff roster reads like a who's who of the sport: Don Carter, Joe Joseph, Marion Ladewig, Carmen Salvino, and Buzz Fazio, to name a few.

In 1954 Brunswick's sales totaled $33 million with only $700,000 of that (4.7 percent) representing profit. Seven years later

tioned adult male league bowlers. Fifteen years later the Women's International Bowling Congress (WIBC) peaked at 4.2 million. Although those numbers have since slid, today's statistics remain impressive. In fact, it's by a significant margin that the WIBC still retains its status as being the largest women's sports organization on the planet.

In addition to being a major sponsor of the pro tours, Brunswick has often staged headline-grabbing events. For example, recently Mike Aulby, Walter Ray Williams Jr., and Randy Pedersen participated in the golf-inspired big-money bowling "Skins Game" at the Villages in Florida. And, Brunswick sponsored a tournament, probably the first-ever outdoor

those figures had swollen to $422 million and $45 million (9.4 percent). The boom lasted through 1961. With 125,000 lanes dotting the American landscape, there were many who projected continued unbridled growth. While the glut of centers gave the impression of a booming industry, few were enjoying a high rate of return on the investment. The following year the effects of market saturation were felt. Nevertheless, automation had brought bowling to a level of popularity that never would have been possible if the sport had remained reliant on pinboys.

ABC membership reached its high-water mark in 1963–64. At that point there were just under 4.6 million sanc-

bowling event in modern times, played in the middle of New York City's Bryant Park. Years before, the Brunswick Shootout included a top amateur player (Chris Barnes), a star from the ladies' tour (Lisa Wagner), and two premier names from the Professional Bowlers Association (PBA), Mark Roth and Marshall Holman.

Today, Brunswick operates hundreds of state-of-the-art centers from coast to coast, in addition to producing all kinds of equipment. The era of the corporate-run center has seen AMF following suit, with its showcase $6 million Chelsea Piers Bowl, part of an enormous sports complex built literally above the Hudson River on Manhattan's West Side.

FROM LEFT: PRESIDENT HARRY S. TRUMAN ON THE COVER OF *KEGLER* MAGAZINE; BABE RUTH TRYING TO STRIKE; BOB HOPE AND FELLOW COMEDIAN JERRY COLONNA EXPERIMENT WITH BOWLING BALLS.

Bowlers Journal International, founded in 1913, is America's oldest monthly sports magazine. With circulation in more than one hundred countries, it has vast influence on the worldwide bowling industry.

BJI was the brainchild of David A. Luby, an immigrant from Ireland who settled in Chicago around the turn of the century. A smooth talker, he soon found a job as a traveling salesman for the Wells Shoe Company. He was also an excellent bowler and billiardist and spent most of his long nights on the road bowling pot games and hustling pool.

Like most bowlers of this and every other age, Dave was frustrated by the lack of bowling coverage in daily newspapers. So, in 1913, he started America's very first consumer sports magazine, the *Bowlers Journal*.

Dave wasn't much of a writer, but it was obvious from the first eight-page issue that this new periodical would be lively and comprehensive. His little magazine tackled all sorts of issues (the lead-loaded "dodo ball" was a big problem at the time) and covered tournaments all over the country. (One of the early issues, from 1924, is shown at right.)

Dave hoped that his two sons Morton and Forrest would eventually take over the magazine. But Forrest caught a lungful of mustard gas during World War I and died soon after his return to Chicago. Mort, however, survived his stint in France with the horse marines and promptly went to work at the *Bowlers Journal* office over the Stock Yards Press.

He was a great traveler who hopscotched across the United States by DC-3 and automobile to interview the game's heros and cover their exploits. He spent one hundred days every year at the American Bowling Congress Championships—filing literally millions of words to the Associated Press and hometown newspapers. At one point, he was Western Union's biggest media client.

He was also one of the first people in the bowling industry to understand the potential of the foreign market. He went to Germany to cover an international bowling exhibition during the 1936 Olympics, which, he hoped, would lead to bowling's eventual inclusion in the Olympic Games. Although bowling still has not managed to obtain permanent status in the Olympics, today there are six thousand tenpins bowling centers in overseas markets (Japan is the largest with eleven hundred establishments), and the Bowling World Cup, for example, has visited more than thirty overseas cities since its inauguration in Ireland in 1965. The Federation Internationale des Quilleurs, bowling's worldwide governing body, runs a massive week-long tournament every four years, which draws participants from some eighty nations.

So, much of Morton's vision of bowling as an international sport has become reality. We can attribute the most recent spurt of overseas excitement to the American pro bowling tours that receive wide television coverage in Asia, Europe, and Latin America. But this media attention would probably never have come about without the first pioneering efforts at covering the sport in print. Today the pages of *Bowlers Journal International* are filled with stories from this rich matrix of competition and will undoubtedly continue to grow along with the sport in this century.

AT THE END OF PROHIBITION BREW-ERIES BEGAN SPON-SORING TEAMS, WHICH LED TO THE EMERGENCE OF THE FIRST BOWLING SUPERSTARS. *CLOCK-WISE FROM TOP LEFT:* DON CARTER, JOE NORRIS, BUZZ FAZIO; THE STROH'S TEAM; THE PABST BLUE RIBBON TEAM; THE STROH'S TEAM; THE BUDWEISERS TEAM.

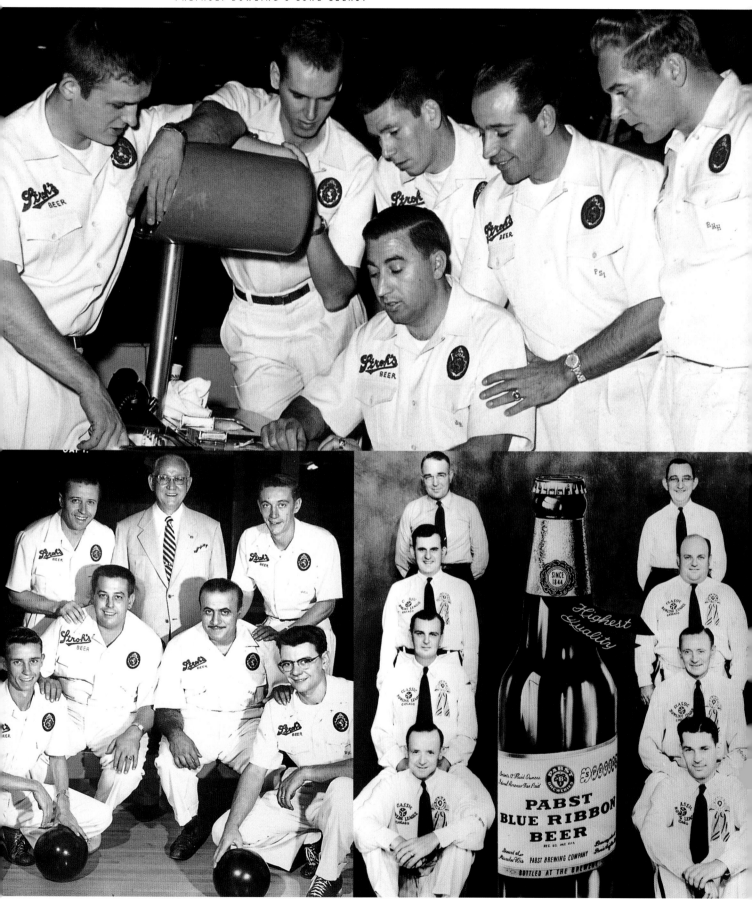

BOWLING PIONEERED THE WORLD OF TELEVISED SPORTS WITH SHOWS LIKE MILTON BERLE'S *JACKPOT BOWLING* (TOP) IN THE FIFTIES, AND LATER WITH EVENTS SUCH AS THE FIRESTONE TOURNAMENT OF CHAMPIONS. ONE OF THE MOST MEMORABLE IMAGES IN SPORTS HISTORY IS THAT OF A PROSTRATE DON JOHNSON AFTER A STUBBORN 10-PIN COST HIM A PERFECT GAME IN THE 1970 FIRESTONE (BOTTOM).

SUDS AND STRIKES AND STARS

When Prohibition officially ended under President Franklin Roosevelt in 1933, major breweries virtually trampled over one another in a rush to sponsor the nation's best bowling teams. Before Prohibition, bowling alleys were dependent on the sales in their bars for survival. The breweries saw in bowling a perfect marketing opportunity, and the connection between the game and brewskies seemed a natural. Stroh Bohemian Brewery in Detroit was the first to assemble a team, captained by Joe Norris, which went on to win the 1934 ABC tournament. Other company-sponsored teams followed after executives witnessed the enormous publicity generated by Stroh's. The most famous of these were the St. Louis Budweisers. Their mind-boggling 3,858 series in 1958 held up as a record for decades even after scoring standards dramatically soared. Their roster included some of the all-time greats: Dick Weber, Don Carter, Ray Bluth, Pat Patterson, Tom Hennessey, and Bill Lillard. Another perennial powerhouse were the St. Louis Falstaffs of Billy Welu, Harry Smith, Glenn Allison, Steve Nagy (for whom the PBA's sportsmanship award is named), Buzz Fazio, and Dick Hoover.

The Stroh's team marked the beginning of a long career for Joe Norris. He is best known for beating Father Time. In 1992 in Corpus Christi, Texas, he surpassed Bill Doherman's career ABC tournament record of 109,398 pins. Joe first rolled in that event in Toledo in 1926. Except for a four-year sabbatical from 1942–46, Norris was a fixture at every ABC. He concluded the twentieth century having toppled 123,770 pins. To put it another way, if you laid those pins end to end, they would span the English Channel—with room to spare. Now well into his nineties, Joe is admired for having managed to compete at the highest levels of the sport decades after his contemporaries had restricted their bowling activities to spectating.

In the year the Stroh's reigned, four of the top six teams were brewery-backed. Blatz finished fourth with Schlitz fifth and Pabst in sixth. In 1939 no less than twenty-six of the top one hundred finishing squads were suds sponsored. The year before, the sponsor list included a squad that represented the famed Manhattan restaurant owned by heavyweight boxing legend Jack Dempsey.

Babe Ruth was also an avid tenpins player during his free time. Bowling's celebrity connection has seen diverse Americans grace the covers of tenpins publications: President Harry S. Truman, former chief justice Earl Warren, and Hollywood icons Mickey Rooney, Bob Hope, and Ronald Reagan. Truman had two lanes installed in the basement of 1600 Pennsylvania Avenue, and at that time there were no less than fifty-eight centers in Manhattan, including seven that operated around the clock. Publicity photos showed the quintessential American couple of the 1950s—Ozzie and Harriet Nelson—rolling strikes.

Such was bowling's popularity during the late 1950s that several TV series were aired, from *Championship Bowling* to *Bowling for Dollars* to *Make That Spare*. The man widely hailed as "Mr. Television," Milton Berle, hosted *Jackpot Bowling*. The show's highlight came the day after New Year's in 1961, when Detroit's Therman Gibson calmly rolled six consecutive strikes to walk off with $75,000. More and more the drama of player-against-player or player-against-pins was filling the airways and captivating viewers.

GOING SOLO

The era of team bowling supported by breweries lasted one generation. Then the launching of the Professional Bowlers Association altered the sport's primary professional focus from group to individual competition. The PBA was the brainchild of the late Eddie Elias, who invited the sport's top performers to a meeting during the 1958 ABC Masters championship in Syracuse, New York. Thirty-three of them became founding members of the PBA. Convincing superstars Carter and Weber to join the fold gave the organization credibility even before the first shot was rolled the following year.

The tour began modestly, with three events in 1959 doling out all of $49,500 in prize money. Lou Campi made $2,500 for winning the first event in Albany, New York. Weber, at $7,672, edged out Bluth and Carter for the initial earnings crown. Two years later legendary sports announcer Chris Schenkel was behind the microphone as ABC-TV aired its first title round of a PBA tournament. A thir-

that professional bowling faced a huge handicap vis-à-vis other sports. Whereas baseball and football could be played in front of tens of thousands of spectators, bowling's live gate was inherently limited. Finding an alternate source of revenue was a must.

It was Elias who sold the Firestone Tire and Rubber Company on the concept of backing the PBA's marquee event by buying time on the telecast and greatly upping the prize fund. In exchange, the sponsor was identified with the competition. In 1965 the Firestone Tournament

teen-week series in 1962 launched one of the longest and most-watched series in the annals of network television. By 1970 the PBA's regional program caught on, giving PBA members all across America the opportunity to compete over the course of a weekend without having to leave their geographical area. It has proven to be a very good training ground for young pros looking to make the transition to the national tour.

The PBA's growth owed much to the Akron-based attorney who gave it its start. Elias's genius lay in understanding

of Champions was born. Elias's stroke of marketing genius has since been copied by several other sports organizations.

The PBA boasted impressive TV ratings, and became the perfect lead-in to Wide World of Sports, providing that show with a sizable carryover audience. Long-time ABC Sports president Roone Arledge championed the move to elevate the profile of his network's Saturday afternoon fare, assigning veteran Chris Schenkel to call the shots. The tournaments set many precedents that would later shape how many other sports would

ABOVE: IN THE SIX-TIES, THE FLEDGLING PBA CULTIVATED MANY OF BOWLING'S GREAT-EST STARS. AMONG THEM WAS FORMER BASEBALL PITCHER EARL ANTHONY, WHO JOINED THE PRO TOUR IN 1969. WITH FORTY-ONE TITLES WON, HE STILL HOLDS THE PBA RECORD.

THE SATURDAY EVENING POST

n Illustrated Weekly
d A.D. ... by Benj. Fran

March 15,
1941
VOLUME 213, NUMBER

5c.
IN CANADA

BOWLING MAKES THE
COVER OF ONE OF
AMERICA'S MOST POP-
ULAR PERIODICALS.

be presented on TV in the years to come.

The drama of four sudden-death games in a ninety-minute time frame was the lure. No game was more riveting than the Dick Ritger–Don Johnson duel during the title match of the 1970 Firestone Tournament of Champions. Ritger rolled a remarkable 266 but it wasn't enough. With eleven straight strikes, Johnson needed one more to claim ten thousand dollars—and the distinction of achieving perfection in his sport's showcase event. But a stubborn 10-pin didn't cooperate, and the resulting photo of a prone Johnson now ranks among bowling's most memorable images. Small wonder that for years PBA's Nielsen statistics easily eclipsed many sports telecasts by comfortable margins.

The PBA's top stars soon became household names. A baseball pitcher whose career was cut short by injuries made the transition to throwing his strikes underhanded. Although he didn't capture his first PBA title until he was thirty-two, Earl Anthony went on to win forty more times, which is still the PBA record. He was honored as the Player of the Year six times in a ten-year span that began in 1974.

While Earl's delivery was as smooth as silk, his chief rival at that time, Mark Roth, had more movements than a Swiss watch. With seven short, choppy steps and a high backswing, Roth's style bore no resemblance whatsoever to any of the players who had preceded him. But four Player of the Year awards and thirty-four titles proved his merit.

More recently, Walter Ray Williams Jr. (a five-time Player of the Year), Pete Weber, Mike Aulby (who holds the record for the highest earnings in any one year), Norm Duke, Brian Voss, and Amleto Monacelli (the first foreign player to be inducted into the Hall of Fame) have risen to the fore. They are the dominant players in a lineage that dates back to legends such as Joe Norris, Hank Marino, and Ned Day (whose elegance on and off the lanes made him the Cary Grant of bowling during the fifties). Their

achievements were carried forth by the likes of Billy Hardwick, Dick Ritger, Don Johnson, Johnny Petraglia, Mike Durbin, Marshall Holman, and Dave Davis.

There was a time, not long ago, when some doubt arose as to whether or not men's professional bowling would survive. The PBA's longtime run on ABC-TV during the prime January through April time frame on Saturday afternoons gave way to two springs on CBS, during which time the PBA seriously went into the red. With dwindling ratings and shrinking fields and prize funds, skeptics questioned the organization's future.

Such sentiments were laid to rest in March 2000, when a group of Internet giants led by former Microsoft VP Chris Peters purchased the PBA. Also investing were Mike Slade, Starwave's former president, and RealNetworks chairman Rob Glaser. Glaser had constructed two lanes in the basement of RealNetworks' headquarters in Seattle. Peters, himself an avid bowler, told the *New York Times*, "We see it as a diamond in the rough, a turnaround opportunity that people were missing. We were so excited that we hoped nobody else would figure it out." Their resources, coupled with strategies for exploiting the marketing potential of cyberspace, assured the sport of a future that promises to eclipse all that has been accomplished to date.

A SPORT FOR BOTH SEXES

Long before Billie Jean King's celebrated straight-sets tennis conquest of avowed sexist/hustler Bobby Riggs in 1973, bowling held its version of the Battle of the Sexes. Floretta McCutcheon was a matronly looking thirty-nine-year-old housewife from Colorado. She had been bowling for less than three years when she was pitted against Brooklyn match-game stalwart Jimmy Smith in 1927. He won round one, 680–672, but she claimed the next series, 704–697. Smith immediately hailed his conqueror as "the greatest bowler I've ever seen." Mrs. Mac, as Floretta McCutcheon came to be known, embarked on a fifty-one-city tour and

TOP: AROUND 1900, BOWLING WAS ONE OF THE FEW SPORTS CONSIDERED APPROPRIATE FOR WOMEN TO PLAY. *BOTTOM:* FLORETTA MCCUTCHEON ("MRS. MAC") WON BOWLING'S BATTLE OF THE SEXES IN 1927 WHEN SHE BEAT THE WELL-KNOWN PLAYER JIMMY STALWART IN A NECK AND NECK SERIES.

went on to spend the better part of the next decade putting on exhibitions. She also opened the Mrs. McCutcheon School for Bowling Instructions. It has been estimated that her organization taught between 300,000 and 500,000 women how to bowl.

While Elias was getting the men's tour off the ground, a meeting was held during the 1959 World's Invitational in Chicago that produced twenty-three charter members for the fledgling Professional Woman Bowlers Association ("Woman" was later changed to "Women's"). More than one hundred players entered the inaugural tournament, held in Miami in September 1960 with the legendary Marion Ladewig pocketing the thousand-dollar first-place

to but five in 1969, a player mutiny led her to resign.

The PWBA eventually gave way to the Ladies Pro Bowlers Tour, and then the original acronym PWBA returned in the 1990s. Having made significant strides of late, women's pro bowling has produced its share of stars. Foremost on the list are Aleta Sill, the first female pro to top the $1 million career official earnings barrier; four-time Player of the Year Lisa Wagner; Wendy Macpherson, widely credited as the top woman bowler of the 1990s; and Donna Adamek, Betty Morris, and Judy Soutar. Other current top performers include Kim Adler, the 1991 Rookie of the Year who won her tenth pro title in 1998; Anne Marie Duggan, who was the first PWBA mem-

NO.	NAME	GAMES	WON	LOST	PINS	POINTS	EX PT
1	M.LADEWIG	32	24	8	6767	159-17	
2	S.WENE		20	12	6403	148-03	
3	R.JENSEN		19	13	6276	144-26	
4	C.POWERS		16½	15½	6286	142-11	
5	H.HOSTA		18	14	6082	139-32	
6	A.SCHUCH		18	14	6025	138-25	
7	P.STREIBECK		14½	17½	6169	137-44	
8	D.KNECHTGES		15	17	6143	137-43	
9	F.ARGENT		16½	15½	6049	137-24	
10	S.BALOGH		13½	18½	6058	134-33	
11	V.MIKIEL		14	18	5989	133-39	
12	E.TOEPFER		14½	17½	5959	133-34	
13	M.GRAHAM		14	18	5965	133-15	
	H.DUVAL		14	18	5952	133-02	

ABOVE, FROM LEFT: ONE OF THE BREWERY-SPONSORED WOMEN'S TEAMS; MARION LADEWIG POINTS OUT HER WINNING SCORE; DON CARTER AND LADEWIG, THE BOWLING STARS OF THE FIFTIES AND SIXTIES.

check. That seemed only appropriate, since ten-time BWAA (Bowling Women's Association of America) Bowler of the Year Ladewig had won eight of the first ten chapters of the old BPAA (Bowling Proprietors Association of America) Women's All-Star event.

While the PBA had found its niche quickly, the women weren't nearly as fortunate. Only one event was held the following year with the "tour" expanding to three tournaments in 1962. The PWBA's growth continued to lag far behind that of the PBA. During its initial decade founder and executive director Georgia Veatch ran the organization out of the bedroom of her home. When the schedule was halved from the ten events of 1968

ber to win a national event as her debut in 1983; Nikki Gianulias; Carolyn Dorin-Ballard; and Carol Gianotti-Block. They have inherited the mantle from such legends as Patty Costello, who won the BPAA U.S. Open three times and dominated play in the seventies, and Dotty Fothergill, who won the BPAA Women's All-Star event back to back in 1968–69 and the WIBC Queens event in 1972–73 back to back.

CASH, CASH, CASH

Big-money events aren't confined to pros. Hundreds of so-called amateurs earn their living with their bowling balls. They all owe a big thank you to a man named Petersen. The next time you're tempted to lodge a complaint with your proprietor over the lane conditions, hold your tongue and be thankful that a time machine hasn't sent you back to roll in the Petersen Classic. In 1921 Louie Petersen first hosted the event offering the outrageous first prize of one thousand dollars, which at the time was a great windfall. To put into perspective the attractiveness of such an amount, consider that the average annual American income at the time was around seven hundred dollars. Given that traditionally bowling has appealed primarily to the working class, it's quite likely that Petersen's bonanza represented two years' worth of accumulated wages to the typical entrant.

With ample public skepticism over his ability to deliver on such a figure, Petersen placed it in escrow. There was but one problem with the qualifying rounds; the required high scores made it unrealistic for Joe Bowler to dream of striking it rich. So, ever the clever entrepreneur, Petersen decided to make scoring difficult in order to entice the masses. Of course, he came up with ingenious methods of increasing the difficulty of rolling high scores. Stories of what was done to squash scoring at Petersen's graveyard have undoubtedly been exaggerated with the passing of time, but one credible report claims that pins were "stored" for a year on the roof of the center, where they were subjected to the ravages of Chicago's notorious winters. There was also a doorman who turned a very nice profit year after year by approaching neophytes from out of town and betting them that they couldn't top a 175 average during their stay.

Over the years megabucks tournaments have evolved considerably: the High Roller tournament is held several times yearly in Las Vegas, attracting thousands of hopeful winners, and the Hoinke Classic was the sport's first $1 million event. The first prize in the amateurs tournaments of today typically totals in the hundreds of thousands of dollars.

BOWLING TODAY

Bowling today is enjoyed in virtually every nation on the planet. It's estimated that about sixty million Americans annually take to the lanes on at least one occasion. At the close of the twentieth century, 3.9 million sanctioned league participants tested their skills in 6,400 centers that contained nearly 130,000 lanes. Presiding over the sport as official domestic governing bodies are the Wisconsin-based American Bowling Congress, the Women's International Bowling Congress, and the Young American Bowling Alliance. With more than a hundred member nations, the

Federation Internationale des Quilleurs oversees bowling on a global basis.

Not everyone plays the same game. Famed New York Giants baseball manager John McGraw was the co-owner of Baltimore's Diamond Bowling Alleys, which introduced small pins to be used when six-inch balls were being rolled. McGraw, an avid hunter, remarked that the trajectory of the little pins flying reminded him of a flock of one of his favorite game birds. Thus the name duckpins was bestowed upon the far lower-scoring version of the sport in which

ABOVE: CURRENT BOWLING CENTER ARCHITECTURE HAS TAKEN ON A STREAMLINED, HIGH-TECH LOOK.

contestants try to topple all ten of their targets. In New England another variant form still thrives; candle-pins involves a softball-sized hard ball, lesser scores, and three-frame shots. Other, more radically different variations exist around the world, but most Americans take aim at fifteen-inch-high pins.

Bowling as a form of recreation is flourishing. The advent of bumper bowling, which involves inflatable tubes placed in both gutters, has made the initial experiences of our younger participants far more fun and rewarding. And, bowling has taken a hip edge with the glow-in-the-dark bowling craze. Open play is thriving.

But bowling as a sport is what continues to fuel the industry. Intercollegiate play is on the rise both quantitatively and qualitatively. While bowling has always been a popular pastime on America's campuses, in recent years it has become a burgeoning sport. Many of today's top pro stars owe much of their development to intercollegiate competition; several institutions now offer bowling scholarships. It's heartening to see our top youth players able to defray parts or all of their university costs thanks to scholarship dollars.

One of the largest participatory annual sporting events in the world is the ABC National Tournament. It's centennial celebration in 2001 commemorates the initial four-day gathering in Chicago, which drew forty-one five-player teams. Tournaments in the last decade typically include about fifty thousand players each year, with the total prize fund usually in the neighborhood of $2 million.

When the WIBC equivalent in St. Louis in 1916 was won by the hometown Progress team, the team had to defeat all of seven rivals to claim the trophy. However, if you plan to roll in that event today, know that you will be a part of the largest women's sporting event on the planet, and you will be facing about forty thousand foes, with $1 million on the line.

Perhaps the most exciting news is bowling's global popularity. The game is growing rapidly overseas, particularly throughout Asia. The Japan Cup is televised and many exhibitions are held leading up to the tournament, which are very popular spectator events.

It was former Brunswick CEO Jack Reicherts's long-standing contention that bowling's image as a legitimate athletic endeavor would only be enhanced if it could be included in the highest-profile international multiple-sport competition; he led an industry-wide push to add ten-pins to the Olympic program. Thanks in large part to the tireless campaigning of Reichert, bowling made its debut as an exhibition sport in the 1988 Olympic Games.

Many unfounded press reports notwithstanding, bowling did not make its Olympic debut that year. That distinction belongs to the infamous 1936 games, the same year American hero Jesse Owens had dominated the track and field scene. In Berlin a forty-lane center was constructed with seating for thirty thousand spectators. After the bowling events concluded the lanes were removed to make way for boxing and fencing. With swastikas everywhere, what was actually the International Bowling Congress Tournament was billed as an Olympic exhibition though technically it was not formally part of the Olympics. One of the five American teams that entered won. They were led by Ned Day and Hank Marino with Norris's squad twelve pins back. Americans won every event except singles, which was claimed by the host nation's Otto Goldhammer.

Besides its two Olympic appearances, bowling has in recent years made great strides toward being accessible for spectators in an arena venue. Some of the greatest moments my peers have enjoyed have come in front of crowds whose enthusiasm and sheer size would have shocked PBA founder Eddie Elias. Arena bowling kicked off in 1994, when a standing-room-only gathering of five thousand fans packed the Erie Civic Center in Pennsylvania to watch a PBA event. The concept of host proprietors

ABOVE: GLOW-IN-THE-DARK COSMIC BOWLING BRINGS A HIP AND FUN EDGE TO BOWLING AS ENTERTAINMENT.

Getting your child off to a positive start with bowling will help to establish a pastime that provides a lifetime of enjoyment. As the father of two sons who look forward to their trips to the lanes, I know that having fun is what counts.

Bumpers are a great invention since watching pins fall is a lot more fun than seeing balls disappear into gutters. However, the flip side is that many kids who are old enough to aim instead just fling their balls without any care about where they go. One solution is to introduce a game I played with my sons—we call it "Bohn's Bumperless Bonus Bonanza."

A shot that never touches the bumper is a bonus ball. The total of these shots is multiplied by the game's score to produce a grand total. For example: Bowler A shoots a 122 while Bowler B has an 86. But Player B had eight clean shots while all but four of Bowler A's shots nudged a bumper. Player B wins 688 (86 x 8) to 488 (122 x 4).

The natural way for a very young child to begin is to push the ball while kneeling down. That leads to standing while rolling with two hands from between the legs to, perhaps, a two-handed sideways throw or forward push. Eventually, the fingers are inserted into the ball.

By the time your child is ready for the "final step," he or she has probably become fairly proficient with the two-handed method. If bumpers aren't being used that means that, at first, scores will likely drop. This can be especially discouraging for a child who is naturally competitive. When the child begins contemplating bowling with one hand only, make sure to offer some encouraging words. For instance, you might mention that while at first scores will decrease,

soon your child will be bowling like a "big" person and a "real" bowler.

From about age three onward a few children are physically and mentally ready to put their fingers into a six-pound ball. One of my sons first did so at age five, while the other was still using both hands at age eight. Don't push your kids, let them decide when they're ready. Through trial and error your kid will discover which hand he or she prefers to bowl with. Until then, I recommend that the ball be drilled with identical finger holes. Correct ball weight is also important. A ball that is too heavy will place stress on developing joints and one that is too light will be flung, not rolled. Between eight and twelve most youngsters should have a ball whose weight equals their age.

Owing to economics, many parents are tempted to make the jump from a ten- to a fourteen-pound ball so that it will last longer. I urge you never to make more than a two-pound increase so that balance and timing aren't harmed.

The final big step is the transition from a conventional to a fingertip grip. That should only come after one is comfortably averaging at least 150. While the amount of hook and carrying power is improved, accuracy suffers. Far too many people go to a fingertip grip before they are ready. Thus they never develop the key fundamentals that will allow them to enjoy greater long-term success.

THE NATIONAL
BOWLING STADIUM IN
RENO, NEVADA.

George and Nancy Warren won kudos, but the cost of transporting and assembling temporary lanes in an auditorium remains so considerable that the idea has not yet taken root.

Just under eight thousand fans rocked Detroit's Joe Louis Arena to see Dave Husted capture the 1995 BPAA U.S. Open. But the nod for the most memorable site has to go to the venue that was used on the first weekend of May 1999. With Mayor Rudolph Giuliani rolling out the ceremonial opening shot, the New York City PBA Experience officially began on the two specially installed Brunswick lanes in Bryant Park, surrounded by the world's third-largest library and skyscrapers on all sides. For the record, his Honor (ironically) went

left of center on his delivery and left the 1-3-8-10 combination (chief executives of major metropolises, apparently, are not required to shoot their spares).

While arena bowling normally involves a temporary construction of four lanes, there is a permanent facility that is the sport's answer to Yankee Stadium and the Rose Bowl. In 1995 the $47.5 million National Bowling Stadium was opened in Reno, Nevada, to stimulate tourism. Having hosted scores of events since it opened, the stadium features eleven hundred permanent seats overlooking eighty state-of-the-art lanes, a giant scoreboard, and a forty-two-foot-high ceiling. Its distinctive eighty-foot aluminum dome, which resembles a silver bowling ball, is visible from miles away. The stadium has been

hailed by *Time* magazine as "the Taj Mahal of ten-pins."

Not all bowling events are so serious. College bowling has helped to launch one of the more zany tube offerings. Aided by colorful commentary from PBA star Randy Pedersen, the Nashville Network's Rockin' Bowl has something for everybody. In addition to rolling a regular Baker-format game, two college teams gain bonus points by attempting to topple pins using such unorthodox methods as swinging the ball while seated in a lounge chair. The popular series kicked off with 900-shooters Vince Wood and Jeremy Sonnenfeld.

As off the wall as that show's antics are, they pale compared to those invented by a certain late-night talk-show host. David Letterman had his guest Dick Weber take to a New York City side street and attempt to topple objects ranging from full beer bottles to lava lamps. Yes, bowling on TV has taken a rather interesting path since the days when the Raccoons squad was led by Ed Norton and Ralph Kramden.

From *The Honeymooners* of the 1950s to *The Drew Carey Show* and countless movies, bowling as an integral part of the American landscape and culture is forever being reinforced by Hollywood. Recently, in *Girl, Interrupted*, a late-night escape to the basement lanes of an asylum provided the patients with their only moments of unbridled joy. And in the classic *The Odd Couple*, when lovelorn bachelor Oscar Madison begged for a night out, Felix Unger took him to the lanes. Other light fare in recent years included *Greedy*, starring Michael J. Fox, *The Big Lebowski*, and *Kingpin*.

What will the future bring for bowling? More technical innovations, to be sure. But the aphorism "the more things change, the more they stay the same" is sure to apply. People have always relished the challenge of attempting to topple objects with an accurately tossed projectile. That should continue for as long as people inhabit the earth.

LEFT: STEVE BUSCEMI, JOHN GOODMAN, AND JEFF BRIDGES IN *THE BIG LEBOWSKI*. *ABOVE*: BILL MURRAY IN *KINGPIN*.

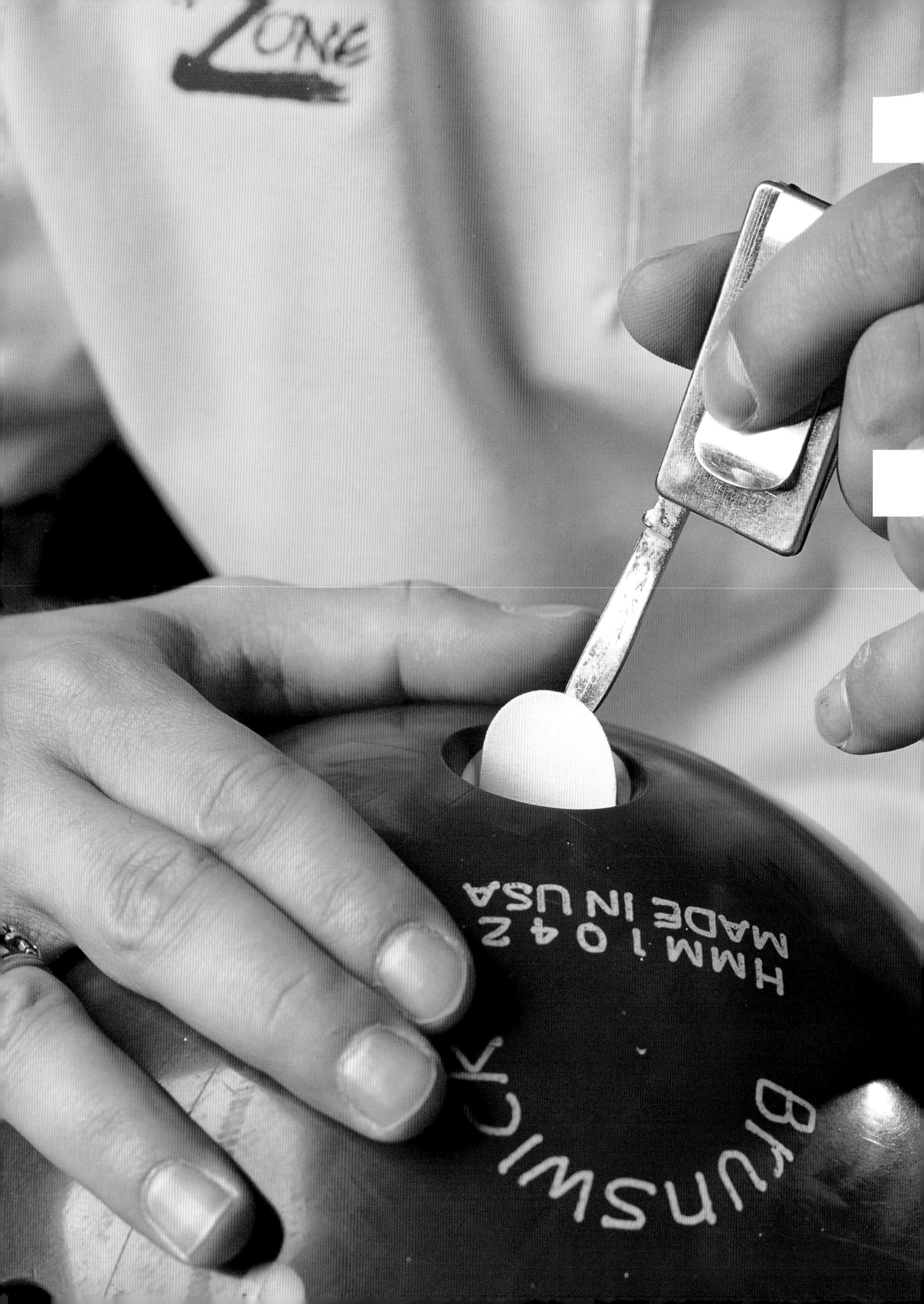
ZONE
HMM 1042
MADE IN USA
Brunswick

CHAPTER ONE: BEING PREPARED

O btaining pointers from this book and subsequently practicing purposefully will make you a better player down the line. If you are reasonably conscientious and have a solid base of natural ability you will likely see positive results within one year. Not so patient? Do you want your money's worth now? Okay, there are some things you can do that will instantaneously upgrade your game. Tops on that list are the steps you ought to take to be fully prepared to perform your best whenever you step onto a bowling lane. I am often shocked by how many of my fellow pros fall short in this regard. I have seen a peer lacking a piece of tape in his bag when thousands of dollars are on the line. Or, he doesn't have any sandpaper on hand prior to the start of a telecast event. Perhaps there is no glue to be found in his arsenal in case a finger or thumb insert becomes loose under the hot television lights. Most of the more successful pros are diligent at paying attention to the so-called little things. We know that should our extra efforts pay off in but one extra strike, the pins gained could spell the difference between achieving our goal or falling just short.

The serious player's preparation begins at the moment just after the final shot was rolled the last time he or she bowled. One of the best-prepared players on the PBA circuit is Eric Forkel. While some lesser pros rush out after a block to replenish their stomachs, the winner of the prestigious 1992 PBA National Championship has a far better postgame routine. Immediately after a competitive game Eric will go through all of his bowling balls to decide which ones he does and doesn't need for the subsequent round. On the ones he will use, he performs any needed adjustments. For example, he may shine one ball (to cut down on its hook) while sanding another (to increase its hook). He could opt to drill some new equipment if nothing in his current arsenal is likely to conquer the lane condition he anticipates facing next. On another ball he might fix the thumb hole, making sure that all of the balls have a similar feel. If you can be one of the handful who is sufficiently prepared before throwing your first shot and before every subsequent shot, you should be able to add ten or more pins to your average game.

PREPARING YOUR EQUIPMENT

Your car's trunk is not for ball storage, especially when weather conditions are extreme; equipment should always be kept at room temperature. Car trunks become saunas in the summer and freezers in the winter. In either case, each ball's surface hardness will be temporarily thrown off kilter. Thus, its characteristics will be distorted upon its first use. The ball that is rock solid from being frozen will skid down the lane, while the one that has "melted" in the heat will hook earlier and more dramatically. Nor will the roll be predictable as the block unfolds, because as the ball adjusts to the center's temperature, it will slowly behave more and more as it was designed to perform. Thus, with each subsequent shot it will hook a bit more (if it had been subjected to being stored in extreme cold) or less (heat). But just how much will it change with each shot? There is no

way of telling. This lack of predictability will make it virtually impossible for you to repeat a successful shot during your first few frames of competition or to make a fruitful adjustment after missing the pocket.

Moreover, placing your hand inside a ball that is either excessively hot or cold can make your fingers and thumb swell or shrink considerably. You will lose the vital "feel" of the ball, and regaining the proper feel could take as long as one or two games. Before you know it, the night is over and you have lost scores of pins unnecessarily.

Even when you manage to keep your ball steady at a room temperature, there are often fluctuations in the temperature of the bowling center and in the temperature of your own body. These you cannot control, but you can help compensate with the use of tape. Chances are that, as a serious player, you own at least a strike ball (or two or more) and another ball for spares (see chapter two, "Knowing Equipment"). Because

feel is vital to executing a smooth and consistent release, every possible step should be taken to bring consistency to the finger- and thumb-hole specs of the balls. Yes, your knowledgeable pro shop proprietor drilled each ball with the same size holes, the same span, and the same pitch. If you're using finger grips or thumb inserts, they too should be identical. But what starts the same doesn't always end up the same. As play unfolds your fingers or thumb might swell or shrink, making it necessary that you add or remove tape from the holes (again, see chapter two). My thumb and fingers tend

EVEN DURING A THREE-GAME SET OF LEAGUE PLAY, YOUR THUMB AND FINGER SIZES ARE LIKELY TO CHANGE.

- MAKE SURE THE BALLS YOU'VE CHOSEN ARE AT ROOM TEMPERATURE AT THE BEGINNING OF A GAME

- ADD OR REMOVE TAPE TO THE HOLES BEFORE PLAY TO KEEP THE FEEL FOR ALL BALLS IDENTICAL

- SAND OR SHINE YOUR BOWLING BALLS AHEAD OF TIME, ANTICIPATING LANE CONDITIONS BASED ON HOW OTHERS' BALLS ARE ROLLING

- KEEP YOUR TOWEL CLEAN TO REMOVE OIL, GRIT, AND DIRT FROM THE BALL

- MAINTAIN A BAG WELL-STOCKED WITH THE TOOLS YOU MIGHT NEED

TAPING: INSERT OR REMOVE TAPE, ON THE SIDE OF THE HOLE THAT TOUCHES YOUR FINGERNAILS.

to swell after one or two games. Thus, by a block's end I often have removed from one to three pieces of tape. Before my subsequent outing I know that my thumb and fingers are likely to be considerably smaller than they were when I concluded play the time before. Thus, my preparation always includes adding as many pieces of tape to each hole as I had to remove during my most recent competitive round.

During the 1997 tour's western swing in March, we went from Los Angeles to Las Vegas. The Brunswick Ice Danger Zone ball that had felt great when I won with it in California's AC-Delco Classic required that all eight pieces of tape be removed once I hit the desert to bowl in the Showboat Invitational—I even had to drill the thumb hole to make it one size bigger. Such were the effects of the difference between Los Angeles's humidity and the dry air of the Silver State. Even during a three-game set of league play, your thumb and finger sizes are likely to change. My recommendation: a few hours before your next trip to the lanes spend the necessary time to add or remove tape from each ball so that the feel of each is identical.

Once you have made sure your bowling balls are suited to you, you want to make sure they are suited for the conditions of the lane you'll be playing on. Let's say that the bowling center tends to have lanes that are extremely dry in the evening (due to constant play all day long, which dissipates the oil) and, thus, hook a lot. If you are rolling with and against high-average players it's quite likely that many of them will opt to shine their balls prior to competition. Doing so decreases friction between the ball and the lane, thus delaying and retarding hook. If you know you'll encounter this situation, I suggest dropping a few quarters into the ball-shining machine before leaving the center after your last match rather than waiting until you arrive for your next appearance, as machines can be broken, the line can be long, or you could be delayed. On the other hand, if

you know you'll be encountering oily lanes, you might want to sand your ball with some sandpaper ahead of time.

One of the vital lessons I first learned after arriving on the tour was the value of scouting the conditions. I identified a handful of fellow left-handed pros whose ball rolls tended to be similar to my own. By watching pros with a break point in the forty- to fifty-foot range like my own I learned a lot. Among these players are Eric Forkel, Mike Aulby, Jason Couch, and John Mazza. My task upon arriving during their final few games of the round is to ascertain where they are playing on the lanes and why. I notice what tends to be successful and which strategies are not rendering the greatest result. Doing so gives me a starting strategy with which to attack the lanes (see chapter six, "Developing Strategies"). It also sometimes means making an equipment adjustment by altering the surface of my ball—by either shining or sanding it.

My bowling towel is cleaned after every tournament. Obviously, my frequency of games greatly exceeds that of the typical amateur player. But, I have seen towels that are so filthy that they looked as if they had just been used to change the oil in a car. You should never allow your towel to reach this point. Wash your towel often enough so that it isn't rubbing dirt or grime into the surface of your bowling balls. I recommend cleaning your ball by holding the towel at opposite ends and buffing the surface of the ball, turning it periodically in the rack to get all sides. You don't want to scrub it with the towel, since that might alter the sanded or shined surface you desire. All you want to do is remove any oil or dirt that has accumulated on the ball in its trip down the lanes and through the ball-return.

Your bag should also include several other helpful implements (see list in the margin). In addition you might want to keep handy a minipack of facial tissues. There will be times when your thumb will become so swollen that it can't exit the ball properly. Drilling the hole larger just isn't a practical on-the-spot solution. What to do? Wrap your bowling thumb in a tissue and jam it into your ball as you wait in the settee area. Remove the tissue before you bowl. Doing this will push the excess water in your hand toward the palm, temporarily shrinking your thumb just enough to help produce a smooth release.

Though I hate smoking with a passion I have managed to find one use for cigarette ashes. When my sliding shoe is sticking on the lane I pick up some ashes from the lounge area's ashtrays and rub some onto the front part of the bottom of

in a warm-up routine you also address an important psychological element by treating bowling as a true sport. This, too, should give you a competitive edge over many of your rivals.

Start by stretching the wrist of your bowling hand. Roll your hand back and forth. In my case, my right (nonbowling) hand grips around my left wrist with the fingers of the left (bowling) hand clinched. Open and close your wrist for several repetitions. Next, stretch your bowling shoulder: reach your bowling arm across your chest, and with your nonbowling hand pull your forearm across your body. Alternatively, extend

- WARM-UP THE WRIST WITH ROTATIONS
- STRETCH OUT THE BOWLING ARM
- LIMBER THE HAM-STRINGS WITH SQUATS
- MAKE THE MOST OF YOUR PRACTICE SHOTS
- PAY ATTENTION TO PROPER BALL PICK-UP

  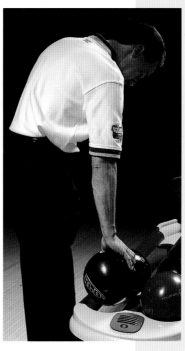

my sliding shoe. Many players use baby powder or a similar substance. However, I prefer ashes, as they will affect only my slide and not that of my fellow players since the ashes blow away quickly and do not leave a residue like baby powder can.

PREPARING YOUR BODY

While bowling doesn't involve the explosive movements demanded of a basketball, football, or soccer player, stretching is still highly recommended. This becomes an even more important consideration as you age and your natural flexibility decreases. Moreover, by engaging

your bowling arm behind your lower back, and with your nonbowling hand firmly grip your bowling wrist. Hold for five to ten seconds to loosen the shoulder and chest. Also, to aid flexibility in the midsection, rotate your torso in clockwise and then counterclockwise directions from the waist, with your hands on your hips or swinging freely.

Next, place your palms against the top of a chair or the ball return apparatus. Lean forward so that your body's weight is supported by your arms. Place one foot near the chair, and the other well behind your body. This will stretch

LEFT: CHECK YOUR SLIDING FOOT FOR STICKING FOREIGN MATERIALS BEFORE YOU STEP ONTO THE APPROACH. *CENTER*: TO PROPERLY PICK UP THE BALL, USE BOTH HANDS, BEND SLIGHTLY AT THE KNEES, AND LIFT USING YOUR LEGS. *RIGHT*: DO NOT USE JUST ONE HAND AND BURDEN YOUR BACK WITH THE WEIGHT.

1. WRIST: SUPPORT THE FOREARM AND CLINCH AND RELEASE WITH THE WRIST OF YOUR BOWLING HAND.

2. WRIST: PRESS THE FINGERS OF BOTH HANDS TOGETHER IN THE CENTER OF YOUR CHEST.

3. ARM: GRAB THE UPPER ARM OF YOUR BOWLING ARM WITH YOUR OTHER HAND AND GENTLY PULL IT ACROSS YOUR CHEST.

4. ARM: GRAB THE WRIST OF YOUR BOWLING ARM WITH YOUR OTHER HAND AND PULL IT TO THE OPPOSITE SIDE OF YOUR BODY.

STRETCHING ROUTINE

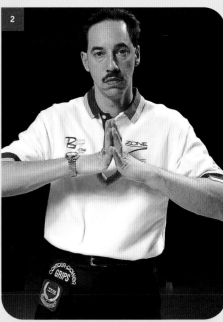

STRETCHING ROUTINE

1. CALF: PRESS YOUR HANDS AGAINST THE BALL-RETURN APPARATUS AND PUSH OUT EACH HEEL BEHIND YOU.

2. LEG: BEND DOWN GRADUALLY INTO A BASEBALL CATCHER'S SQUAT SEVERAL TIMES, WITHOUT BOUNCING.

3. LEG: BEND AT THE WAIST AND TRY TO PRESS YOUR PALMS TO THE GROUND.

4. HAMSTRING: LIFT ONE FOOT TO THE BALL-RETURN APPARATUS AND LEAN FORWARD SLIGHTLY WITH YOUR HANDS CLASPED BEHIND YOUR BACK.

MOST BOWLERS DO NOT APPRECIATE THE IMPORTANCE OF THE LEGS IN THIS SPORT.

FOR YOUR PRACTICE FRAME, ROLL YOUR SPARE SHOT FIRST FOLLOWED BY YOUR STRIKE BALL.

the Achilles tendon in the heel of the back foot. Switch feet and repeat the procedure for five to ten seconds.

Most bowlers do not appreciate the importance of the legs in this sport. Always engage in some squats (that is, imitating a baseball catcher's stance) to limber your legs. Finally, bend forward from the waist with your hands firmly gripping your ankles or, if you can, touch your palms against the floor in front of the toes. Either way, hold the position for about ten seconds and do not bounce—bouncing can damage muscles. This stretch addresses the hamstrings and the lower back. Now that my thirtieth birthday is but a distant memory my palms no longer can reach the floor (or even come close). I just do the best I can by placing them as low as they are willing to go.

Is it absolutely essential that you stretch? No. Many successful players have opted to neglect this aspect of warming up. However, I know that I will be calling upon a lot of specific muscle groups that are not used in everyday activities to perform from my first shot until my last. By preparing them for the task at hand I am convinced that my simple five-minute routine provides me with a competitive advantage while lessening the incidence and severity of any injuries. Avoiding injuries is no minor consideration given that a wrist ailment that would hardly impact a football player could greatly hinder or altogether eliminate a bowler's ability to perform for weeks or even months at a time. More than one big-time player has lost tens of thousands of dollars when a wrist, knee, or shoulder problem put them on the shelf.

There is another huge advantage for the typical league bowler whose body is loose and ready prior to the start of the official warm-up session. Most centers limit teams to five minutes of warm-up time. In a four- or five-player league each individual might get to roll as few as two to four practice shots. If you're not properly stretched out, the first few shots must be rolled gingerly, until the body has become sufficiently flexible to allow for your regular motions. This wastes valuable practice shots that could otherwise be used to learn about lane conditions or experiment with a different release, hand position, strike line, or ball.

Making the most of the finite amount of practice time helps me to gain an edge over less-experienced players. One hint: roll your spare shot first followed by your strike ball. Thus you will always get two shots per turn, while your rival who strikes on his first shot actually loses one delivery. In contrast, the advanced league or tournament bowler who is competing on a high-scoring condition may opt to ignore this hint. He is seeking to determine the best angle, ball speed, roll, and ball surface combination to minimize his margin for error. Thus, he needs to know which strategy is most likely to trip the 4-pin or carry a light hit. This can be accurately ascertained only against a full rack of pins. But whether you're Walter Ray Williams Jr. or a once-a-month enthusiast, making the most of your preparation time will be to your utmost advantage.

Once you are all limbered up, it's important not to tighten up again when you reach to pick up your ball. This may seem like a simple, commonsense task, but so many bowlers do it without thinking and consequently harm the muscles they are about to use in the swing. Don't jerkily lug the ball up using only your arms; this can hurt your back, which could make your swing tense and lead to long-term problems if repeated often. Instead, wrap both hands around the sides of the ball and lift using your leg muscles to pull up the weight.

Most of today's top bowlers view themselves as athletes. You should, too. The self-confidence you will gain by preparing yourself to compete to the best of your ability will provide you with a significant advantage over less-conscientious opponents. I truly believe that a big part of my success owes to positive habits on and off the lanes.

After graduating from San Jose State my ambition was to become a successful athlete. Making Team USA and going to the Olympics were my goals, in large part because doing so earned squad members access to the National Training Center in Colorado Springs, where I'd have the opportunity to improve even more. While there I read as many relevant sports psychology titles I could find. We attended lectures on nutrition. We engaged in weight training. The time spent on the lanes had us being taped by cameras from different angles to more easily identify and correct technical flaws.

That week in residency reemphasized just how important it is to have an athlete's mentality. A player who views himself or herself in that light and then acts accordingly will bowl better and enjoy a longer career. And being an athlete means staying fit. That's why I don't smoke. I drink alcohol in moderation and only at appropriate times. Fried foods are kept to a minimum.

After a series of back, hip, and wrist ailments I hired a personal trainer in 1993. I have been largely free of such injuries since I began working with Karen Sargent twice weekly in San Mateo. We split our ninety-minute sessions between lifting weights and resistance exercises in the pool. Our overall focus is on building leg strength as well as addressing my shoulders and biceps.

A big part of any athletic competition involves the thought process during the heat of battle.

There's no question that one of the major contributing factors in my career has been sports psychologist Keith McConnell. He helped me learn how to remain calm in pressure situations. Through him I have come to view key shots as a positive experience and a challenge to be relished, regardless of the outcome. I now take the healthy perspective that pressure is the reward that one derives for having performed well. Part of learning how to relax involves breathing techniques. I also utilize visualization by picturing a good shot from early in the tournament to replicate the feeling I had when there was minimal pressure riding on that particular ball.

Another positive change that has enabled me to emerge as one of the better players on the PWBA tour involves my practice habits. I now spend less time on the lanes than earlier in my career but every moment of practice incorporates one hundred percent concentration and intensity. For a practice session to be fully useful, you must train with the same determination that one brings to competition. If you have the means, having a long-time relationship with a personal coach is valuable. Because my sister works for United Airlines, I often fly for modest fares to Kansas to work under former Wichita State assistant coach Pat Henry. When changing some aspect of my delivery we will put in a lot of games, as many as twelve per session, until I've gotten the hang of it. But, I rarely bowl for more than ninety minutes to ensure that my level of concentration doesn't falter.

2

I f you wandered into the paddock during a PBA or PWBA event you would hear talk of cover stocks, weight blocks, and pin placements. To a neophyte, it might sound like a discussion of investments, people in dire need of a diet, and a golfing challenge. In reality, these terms refer to bowling balls (we'll get to their definitions soon).

Customizing these and other aspects of the ball to fit your individual game and the lane conditions will help you produce the largest margin of error. Add top-class shoes and a variety of bowling aids, and your margin for error increases even further.

Modern ball technology has become so complicated that many pros rely upon ball-drilling experts to find just the right formula to match the strengths of their game to a specific lane condition.

Equipment has experienced more than an evolution in the relatively short time I've been on the tour—it's really been a revolution. Whereas my boyhood heroes rolled rubber balls that retailed for about thirty bucks, today's players use hi-tech balls that can set them back well in excess of two hundred dollars.

As recently as the early 1970s it wasn't unusual for a pro star to use the same ball on every shot for several weeks at a time. Only when that ball became worn out was it replaced.

Nowadays, the typical pro lugs at least four balls from lane to lane between games, with several more ready in the paddock. For regular bowlers, anyone with an average in excess of 150 should own at least two bowling balls: one for strikes and another used for most spare conversions. (The strike ball will be constructed and drilled to hook while the spare ball will be constructed and drilled to go straight.)

Research and development has progressed at a rapid pace: following from the original wood balls, the game saw balls of rubber, soft rubber, plastics, urethanes, reactive resins, and, most recently, textured urethanes. With each equipment enhancement came new opportunities for bowlers to topple pins more effectively. Balls now roll more consistently and grab lanes better than ever before. Predictably, scores have been soaring at all levels.

Mark Roth's 221.7 average in 1979 made him the first to break the 220 plateau on the PBA tour for an entire year. That standard stood for fourteen years until Walter Ray Williams Jr. managed a 223. Two years later Mike Aulby bettered the 225 barrier. Walter Ray went him one pin better in 1998 and then I came in at over 228 in 1999. To put into perspective just how the environment has changed, the 212.84 average that Don Carter posted to lead the circuit in 1962 was eclipsed by sixty-six players in 1999.

Likewise, Wendy Macpherson's 218.9 established a new PWBA record in 1999. Wendy's average was ten pins higher than Lisa Wagner's tour-setting pace of 1983. The quantity of honor scores produced by amateur and recreational bowlers has also risen at mach speed. In 1974 there were 1,377 recorded perfect games rolled by ABC members, while in 1999 there were a whopping 34,470; the 800 series also rose in this same period from 236 to 8,043. Perfect games have now been rolled by preteens, and it's hard to find even a good local player who hasn't bagged a 750 series.

It's tempting to point to new ball technology as the main cause behind this rocketing rise in scoring, but the bowling ball is only part of the puzzle. So, before you go into a pro shop to make this technology work for you, it's best if you understand a little about the role oil plays on the lane. This is because oil conditions and ball type are always linked.

SLICK ALLEYS

Lane oil is applied in order to protect the front portion of the lane from damage caused by the impact of the bowling balls. Typically, about eighteen milliliters of oil is applied to the surface of each lane at the average bowling center. On the men's tour, it's about thirty milliliters, and on the women's tour, it's about twenty-five milliliters. This is such a scant amount when spread over so much surface area, and thus it is very hard to detect its presence with the naked eye. However, within ABC guidelines, the amount of oil used can vary, as can the distance to which it is applied. The phrase "short oil" is used to describe a lane whose oil coating ends at a short distance down the lane away from the foul line. Then of course "long oil" describes a lane whose coating extends at a longer distance from the foul line. From your first few shots on a lane, you should try to get a feel for the amount and distribution of oil on a particular lane. Then you should adjust your shots accordingly.

Generally speaking, your strike shot will skid through the oiled portion of the lane, much as a car's tires might hydroplane on a wet road. As the ball reaches the more lightly oiled middle of the lane some friction between the ball and the lane surface is encountered and your shot begins a transition phase from skidding to rolling. You can spot this transition by watching your ball's markings to see when they begin turning end over end. Finally, as it enters the dry

IF THE HEADS ARE BECOMING INCREASINGLY DRY AND CAUSING EARLY HOOK AND A WEAK FINISH, TRY LOFTING YOUR SHOTS TWO TO SIX FEET BEYOND THE FOUL LINE.

- OIL IS APPLIED TO LANES IN VARYING DISTANCES AND AMOUNTS
- LONG OIL LANES PUSH THE BALL'S BREAK POINT FURTHER DOWN THE LANE
- SHORT OIL LANES MOVE THE BREAK POINT UP CLOSER TO THE FOUL LINE
- AVOID DRY TRACKS THAT HAVE BEEN WORN INTO THE OIL ON A LANE
- ALWAYS TAKE INTO CONSIDERATION OIL CONDITIONS WHEN CHOOSING A BALL

AFTER 40 GAMES

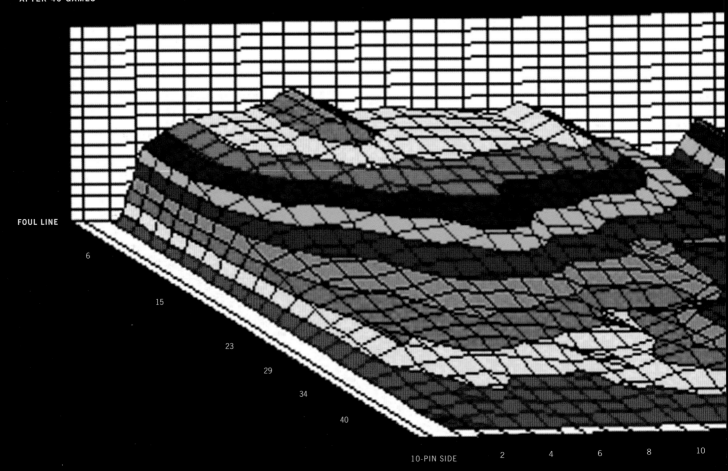

FOUL LINE

6

15

23

29

34

40

10-PIN SIDE   2   4   6   8   10

BEFORE

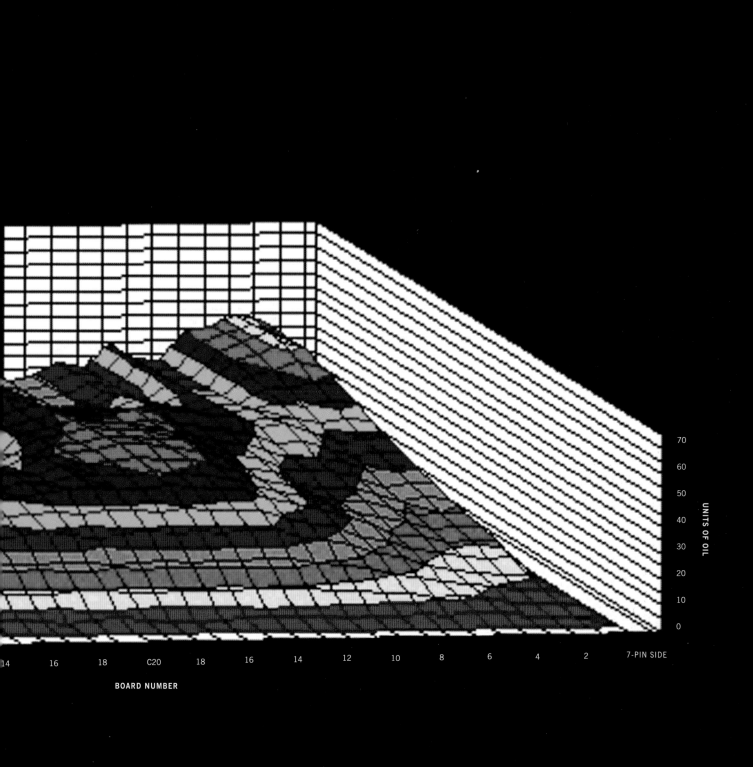

70
60
50
40
30
20
10
0

UNITS OF OIL

14   16   18   C20   18   16   14   12   10   8   6   4   2   7-PIN SIDE

BOARD NUMBER

Just as wooden balls had given way to rubber ones, the sport again changed dramatically following a startling discovery in the mid-1970s by Don McCune. A steady but hardly a great player on the tour, McCune's genius came by irrefutably proving the value of a superior ball.

Although he turned pro in 1964, it wasn't until 1968 that Don entered several national tour events. In the five-year period that followed he won two tournaments and finished anywhere on the yearly earnings list from thirty-sixth to twentieth, with a then career-best of almost $24,000 in 1972. McCune then uncovered a liquid chemical compound that softened the outer shell of his bowling ball and, with that, forever changed our sport. Armed with the soon-to-be-famous so-called soaker ball, he dominated the PBA in 1973. In the middle of the PBA Winter Tour he caught fire, winning five of eleven events. Don finished that campaign with six triumphs and a PBA-best $69,000 en route to being voted the Player of the Year.

Had Don not revealed his secret, he probably would have managed to maintain his competitive edge. McCune's soaker ball prompted bowling authorities to pass legislation that mandated a minimum hardness for all balls. Regulations on size and weight already existed but no one had thought to make strictures on the hardness of the surface. No less than a 72 rating was required on a special scale that's derived when a durometer is inserted into a ball. Meanwhile, both pro tours prohibited the use of any ball with a rating under 75. To ensure fair play, all pros finishing in the money at any event must have their equipment checked by tournament personnel before any paychecks are issued.

With his soaker ball relegated to the scrap heap of bowling history, McCune didn't capture any more events on the national tour. Only when he finished thirteenth in 1974 did he again manage to crack the top-twenty-five earnings list. Nevertheless, his impact was monumental because since that time players and manufacturers alike have been paying special attention to ball surface and the role it plays in performance.

backend even greater friction is encountered and so the ball will hook (if rolled correctly). This is what is called the skid-roll-hook pattern and it will be explored in more detail in chapter four. Although you can strike with a straight ball, a ball that hooks into the pocket is a more fail-safe method because it generates a more powerful hit. The point at which your shot begins to hook is known as your break point. Oil can either shorten or extend your break point. On a long oil lane, your break point will be farther down than usual, whereas on a short oil lane your break point will be closer than usual. It is important that your break point be neither premature nor too late, so you need to take into account oil patterns to keep your break point where it should be.

A ball that begins to hook too soon will expend much of its energy before it reaches the backend. By the time it nears the pins, your ball will have "rolled out." Usually, the result is a weak hit, with the ball deflecting significantly after it contacts the pins. Even a seemingly solid pocket hit could result in a difficult split such as the 5-7 or 8-10 for a right-handed player or the 5-10 or 7-9 for southpaws. On the other hand, when your break point is delayed, the ball comes in behind the headpin. As a result, it's quite likely that a right-handed player would find the 2-pin and/or the 10-pin standing, while a lefty would face a 3-pin and/or a 7-pin. For more information on the ideal strike shot and pocket hit, see page 85.

Another consideration with oil patterns is the fact that as play wears on during a day or evening, the oil distribution on the lanes changes and "breaks down." As each ball rolls down the lane, it will pick up oil, as can often be seen when it returns and you wipe it with your towel. The ball also may dissipate the oil, making it migrate toward one side of the lane. A single strike line that is popular with many bowlers on one lane may wear a track into the oil, so that one line becomes dry. You will want then to avoid this dry line. A dry line or a dry lane

results in considerably greater friction between ball and lane, which may increase the amount of your ball's hook greatly. Since too much hook isn't desirable, you'll want to counter the conditions by rolling a ball that is designed to hook only slightly. The other extreme is what we call a "fresh lane," one which has just been oiled and on which no other bowlers have played yet. Even after some have bowled on it, a lane may still be "wet." These lanes are often best conquered by using a ball that is designed for ample hook, since oil tends to limit your hook.

THE RIGHT BALL FOR THE JOB

When you wander into your pro shop you will be confronted with the most choices this side of a twenty-four-hour diner's menu. Among the questions you must answer: How many balls do I need? How much can I afford to spend? What weight of ball best suits me? What type of grip do I need? What are the strengths and weaknesses of my game? What type of lane condition am I looking to conquer?

The first and most important factor to consider is cover stock, which is the substance of the ball's surface. This is the part of the ball that has had the greatest improvements over the past quarter century; many different types of materials and hardnesses are available. The basic division is between porous and hardshell. The difference between the two lies mainly in their relationship to oil. A ball with a more porous cover stock will generate more contact area between the ball and the lane, giving your ball a greater hook. It's especially useful on "wet" conditions when the lanes aren't hooking a lot. The pores also have the effect of absorbing the oil on the lane and can thus slow down the ball. A ball with a harder shell cover stock will encounter minimal friction, which leads to less of a hook and greater speed. This kind of ball is preferred when you want your shots to go straight, such as for a strike ball on a very dry lane or for shooting spares. All of

- POROUS COVER STOCKS INCREASE HOOK AND DECREASE SPEED

- HARDSHELL COVER STOCKS DECREASE HOOK

- CORE DESIGNS USE DYNAMICS TO EFFECT DIFFERENT TILTS AND HOOKS

- THE PLACEMENT OF THE PIN IN RELATION TO TRACK AND AXIS POINTS AFFECTS FLARE

- LESSER FLARE MEANS A DELAYED BREAK POINT

- GREATER FLARE MEANS A GREATER ARC IN YOUR SHOT

- AN AXIS-WEIGHTED BALL PROVIDES FOR A SMOOTHER DOWN-LANE REACTION

- IT'S ADVISABLE TO USE THE HEAVIEST WEIGHT YOU CAN CONTROL

A MORE POROUS COVER STOCK CREATES
GREATER HOOK, WHILE A HARDER SHELL
COVER STOCK CREATES LESS HOOK AND
GREATER SPEED.

ABOVE AND RIGHT :
MODERN COVER
STOCKS DO A BETTER
JOB OF RESPONDING
TO THE OIL PATTERN
THAT IS APPLIED TO
THE LANE.

today's cover stocks are so well calibrated that they are often able to "forgive" an error such as a subpar release or a lack of power on the appropriate lane condition. And, you can always alter your cover stock toward one direction or the other by sanding, which makes a ball hook more, or by shining, which has the opposite effect.

Oil tends to migrate on synthetic lanes while a natural (wood) surface will absorb some of the conditioner. In general, a higher friction ball is preferred on a synthetic lane while a lower friction ball is more likely to be appropriate most often on wood. However, even geography can play a role. Centers on America's east coast are rarely conducive to using a higher friction ball due to greater humidity. In most such places, your ball will expend too much energy fighting through the head portion of the lanes and will be dead on arrival when it hits the pins.

Once you have reached a serious level in your practice and play (averaging above 150), you will need one ball for strikes and another for most spare conversions. The spare ball has a hardshell cover stock that is designed to go as straight as possible so as to maximize what's required—accuracy—while eliminating what's superfluous—power. Conversely, the strike ball usually has a softer and more porous cover stock. It's drilled so as to hook powerfully into the pocket. There are exceptions when you would want a different strike ball, for instance when you are faced with a very dry condition such as during night blocks on the pro tours or when your style is so powerful as to require modification. Bowlers with averages at or beyond 180 will probably carry at least three balls, including two strike balls—one for oily and one for dry lanes.

A distant second in importance after cover stock is the weight block of the ball. Weight blocks are the mass of inter-

nal materials that affect the ball's tilt and thus where and how your shot starts to hook toward the pocket. Weight blocks come in many different shapes, which are called core designs and can resemble a wide range of objects from a mushroom to a bullet. There are many weight block and core design options, which are forever changing. Your core has a dynamic effect on your strike shots. This can occur only if it revolves as it rolls down the lane. Without revolution there is no dynamic effect. As revolutions increase so does the effect. These subtle considerations are far more significant at my level of the sport, but of course your pro's knowledge can provide you with an edge at any level.

One of the most significant decisions you will have to make involves the weight of your ball. Bowling balls range from as little as six to a legal maximum of sixteen pounds, and their circumference may not exceed twenty-seven inches. I strongly suggest that you use the heaviest weight that you can comfortably control. The greater your ball's weight, the harder it will hit the pins. However, a ball that is too heavy for your level of strength will cause fatigue and a loss of balance and, with it, a loss of accuracy. A ball that is too light could induce a "muscled" armswing, resulting in shots that are flung instead of rolled. If in doubt, however, your needs are far better served by erring on the side of a slightly lighter ball and consistently producing accurate shots than by lugging around a ball that is too heavy.

Most adult males will opt for a sixteen-pound ball, while those over fifty are generally better served by a lighter ball. The typical women's ball ranges from ten to twelve pounds. However, some advanced women bowlers and women with above-average strength can use anything up to and including the maximum legal weight of sixteen pounds.

USE THE HEAVIEST BALL YOU CAN HANDLE SAFELY.

- CONVENTIONAL GRIPS ARE BEST FOR NOVICES AND NONPOWER PLAYERS

- FINGERTIP GRIPS PROVIDE MORE POWER BUT IMPAIR ACCURACY

- PIN PLACEMENT IN RELATION TO YOUR TRACK GREATLY AFFECTS YOUR BALL'S ABILITIES

- POSITIVE WEIGHT INCREASES HOOK; NEGATIVE WEIGHT DECREASES HOOK

- TOP WEIGHT PUSHES THE BREAK POINT FURTHER DOWN; BOTTOM WEIGHT BRINGS IT UP CLOSER

- FINGER WEIGHT PUSHES THE BREAK POINT FURTHER DOWN; THUMB WEIGHT BRINGS IT UP CLOSER

- FORWARD PITCH INCREASES HOOK; REVERSE PITCH DECREASES HOOK

- EXTRA HOLES CAN INCREASE HOOK OR ACT AS A COUNTERBALANCE TO OTHER ADJUSTMENTS

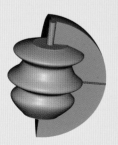

Except for children who are either exceptionally heavy or light for their age, I recommend one pound of ball weight for every year between ages eight and twelve. Extenuating circumstances need to be considered. For example, a youngster who has suffered a fractured arm or a broken wrist might be better served with a lighter ball. Teenage boys often opt for a sixteen-pound ball prematurely; doing so is far better for the macho ego than it is for the scoring average.

At all ages, the key is observation. Is your ball speed comparable to that of most of your peers? If it's too slow your ball might be too heavy. Here's a good test: hold the ball to your side and swing it from your shoulder without releasing it. Can you easily maintain speed and control? Another key: if the shoulder of your bowling arm drops during the downswing your ball could be too heavy. Also, be aware of the fact that if you're using a ball whose grip isn't customized to your hand size, it will feel heavier than a ball that fits you properly.

I believe that as soon as a child is old enough to attend school he or she is old enough to own his or her own ball. Buying a six-pound ball isn't an expensive investment and it's likely to come featuring one of your child's favorite cartoon characters. The benefits include the special feeling of owning one's own ball as well as learning to handle responsibility: having to put it back in the bag after bowling, bringing the bag back to the car, and putting it away in its special place upon returning home.

DRILLING FOR GOLD

Regardless of whether the ball you've just purchased is six pounds and purple with a picture of Snoopy on it, or the top-of-the-line sixteen-pounder, you are able to alter significantly many of its characteristics by deciding how it is to be drilled. First, you need to figure out which kind of grip you want the ball drilled for. Younger and lower-average players should utilize a conventional grip, in which the ball is drilled so that

your fingers are inserted up to the second knuckle into the holes. This will provide for a maximum amount of control. By the teenage years and when a player has become sufficiently accurate and proficient to average 150 or above comfortably, a fingertip or semifingertip grip is an option. A fingertip grip means the ball is drilled so that the fingers are only inserted to the first joint into the ball. With a semifingertip grip the fingers come in at a depth just between the conventional and the fingertip grips. Both the fingertip and semifingertip impart a greater amount of hook and carrying power. However, these grips make accuracy slightly more problematic.

The next basic specification to make in drilling involves your span. Span is the distance between the thumb hole and the finger holes. The pro shop should help you determine the correct span for your hand. If it is too long, your thumb's exit from the ball upon release will probably be delayed. If the span is too short, your ball will have less rotation, which leads to less hook. Keep in mind that your hand may swell or shrink depending on your body temperature and condition. The finger- and thumbholes should be drilled so that they will fit your fingers and thumb when they are at their biggest. That way at all other times you can use tape or insert grips to get a tight fit.

When you are having your ball drilled, the key factor to consider is the positioning of the pin in relation to your ball's track and axis points. When the ball is made the core is supported in the mold on a metal pin. After casting, the metal pin is removed, and the hole that is left is filled with a plug-type material. Thus, in balls with shaped cores the pin tells you the location of the core's center line. If the core's center line is offset slightly from the center of the ball one-sixteenth to one-eighth an inch, the marked center of gravity will move away from the pin. The location of the center of gravity (CG) is shown by a small mark on the surface of the ball. The CG's position is manipulated for weight-hole considera-

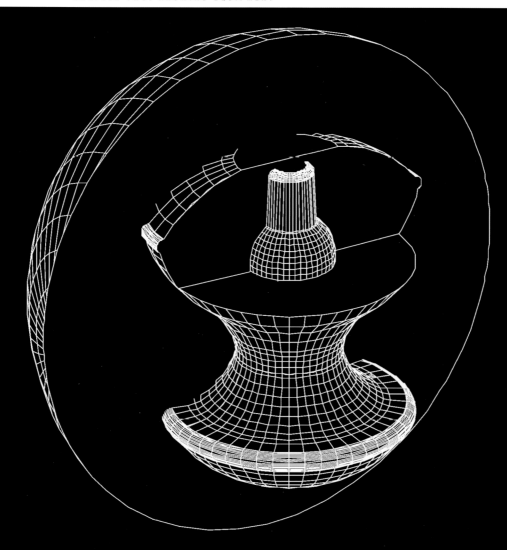

THIS PAGE AND OPPOSITE: CORES THAT CONCENTRATE MORE WEIGHT TOWARD THE CENTER OF THE BALL CAUSE THE BALL TO ROLL EARLIER. CORES THAT CONCENTRATE MORE WEIGHT TOWARD THE COVER OF THE BALL CAUSE THE BALL TO ROLL LATER. CORES THAT ARE MORE CYLINDRICAL HAVE THE POTENTIAL TO CREATE MORE FLARE, DEPENDING ON THE DRILLING.

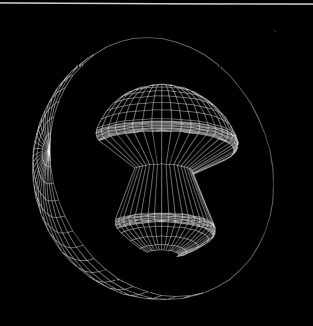

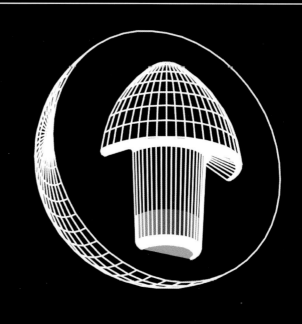

CLOCKWISE FROM TOP:
DANGER ZONE PRO
HPD; VIOLET QUAN-
TUM; THREE-PIECE
DESIGN; QUANTUM
CORE; THREE OTHER
UNUSUAL CORES.

tions. The distance between the marked center of gravity and the pin is called the "pin-out" distance.

As you bowl a succession of games with your new ball, your ball will develop a track. This is the circular ring on the cover that actually comes in contact with the lane. You will be able to identify your track by noticing a circle of oil following a shot. After a ball has been used for several games the track area will exhibit a series of nicks as evidence of wear and tear.

Imagine that as your ball rolls down the lane it has an axle stuck through its center, like the axle connected to the wheels of a car. The two ends of this imaginary axle are called axis points, and the axis point that is closer to the center of the lane (which would be on the ball's left side if it's a right-hander's shot) is called the positive axis point. Your axis points change depending on what you do as you release the ball.

The placement of the pin in relation to the track and axis points affects what is known as flare. You may see that the oil rings fan out on the left or right side of your normal track on the ball's surface—this is flare. Flare is caused by an unstable core position that seeks to become stable in order to make the core tumble end-over-end as it progresses toward the pin deck.

Minimizing flare delays break point and can provide for a stronger down-lane reaction. The ball's down-lane reaction is always relative to several variables. Maximizing flare increases traction between the ball and the lane. This is primarily due to the ball's rotating on a slightly different ring of its outer shell on each successive revolution. Because of this, the previously accumulated oil on the ball that would have reduced traction is not in contact with the surface. Instead, a fresh surface of the ball rolls against the lane so that traction is increased. As a result, on a synthetic surface with heavy oil your ball will react hard, hooking strongly, after reaching the dry portion of the lane. In general, your shots should

grab the lane earlier with a noticeable increase in the size of the shot's arc.

Your flare increases proportionate to an increase in the number of revolutions that you are able to generate. When the pin is on your axis point your ball will have minimal or no flare. As the distance from the pin to the axis point increases so does flare. To maximize flare your pro drills your ball so that the pin is located exactly three and three-eighths inches away from your positive axis point. That precise spot, which provides the maximum flare potential, is known as the leverage point. Once one gets beyond that point, flare will begin to decrease. At six and three-quarters of an inch the flare either will be eliminated entirely or be minuscule.

With each incremental move of the pin comes a subtle change in ball reaction. For example, as the pin moves toward the axis point from the leverage point a progressively smoother down-lane reaction occurs, coupled with an earlier break point. As the pin moves toward the track from the leverage point, the break point is delayed. However, the amount of backend reaction will be predicated upon the combined effects of several other variables. As the pin is now positioned under or near the track area the flare will be no more than slight as the ball's core is in a stable position to allow it to tumble end-over-end. This will cause the shot to have a far more modest change of arc after reaching the break point. Once again, the overall reaction and the shape of the arc pattern will be determined by a myriad of factors.

The equating of all such considerations to produce the optimum reaction for your game and the lane condition on which you most frequently compete requires great expertise. To decrease flare, the pin is moved from the leverage point closer to the track or toward the positive axis point. This will reduce the surface friction that the ball will encounter as it rolls down the lane. The closer that your pin is placed to your track, the later your shot will begin to

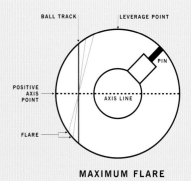

MAXIMUM FLARE

MINIMUM FLARE

hook. This occurs because there is less friction due to the reduced flare.

Whenever the pin is positioned on the positive axis point it is known as an axis-weighted ball. This option provides for a smoother backend reaction with your shots rolling much like a barrel. When this is used, the ball tends not to flip over and snap on the backend and it gets into its roll earlier. Earlier roll/break point can be enhanced by using a weight hole relative to your axis point. Your pro will take special care to note the ball's inner core design since removing material from the ball could cause an adverse effect if done to the wrong part of the ball.

Of course, if the lane heads are heavily oiled and/or you are using a hard-shell ball you will delay the start of your shot's transition from skid to roll. As the distance from the pin to the positive axis point increases (moves closer to your leverage point), overall reaction and/or backend hook will increase.

Keep in mind that all equipment adjustments are relative to your release, the ball's cover stock, and the lane condition. Most top-level players have their pin placed from four-and-a-half to five-and-a-half inches from the positive axis point. This provides for a combination of length (delayed break point) with increased backend reaction for maximum carrying power. In essence, the ball's energy is stored for when it matters the most as it smashes into the pocket.

For the typical league bowler, I suggest having the pin either on the leverage point or up to four-and-a-half inches from your axis point. This will increase track flare. It provides more help for those of you who can't generate as many revs as do I. When to use an axis-weighted ball? My recommendation is for when you wish to smooth out your down-lane reaction. Typically, this would be on freshly oiled lanes whose backends are overreacting. Use a ball whose pin is on or near the track when you want to play straighter on lanes that have very dry front ends.

LESS FLARE CREATES A DELAYED BREAK POINT WHILE MORE FLARE CREATES A STRONG HOOK AND BALL ARC.

TRADITIONAL ADJUSTMENTS

In addition to the above high-tech considerations that delve into the realm of physics, there are other, more traditional options available for how your ball is drilled.

Positive and Negative Weight

Your ball can be drilled so that the center of gravity is slightly offset toward one side of the ball. This alters how it will react to the lane. Imagine drawing a line from twelve o'clock to six o'clock, with the line bisecting your finger holes and your thumb hole. Regulations allow up to one ounce of variance of side weight in either direction, which is measured in a pro shop. So-called positive weight will increase the hooking action. This is when the center of gravity is slightly offset toward the side of the ball that corresponds to your bowling hand. An exception is for players who roll a backup ball. Conversely, negative weight retards the hooking process.

The chances are that like most league and recreational bowlers, you are seeking to throw a more powerful hook. Thus, after watching you in action your pro is likely to drill your strike ball with the maximum amount of permissible positive weight. While this should prove somewhat helpful, the positive versus negative weight consideration is not nearly as important as it was even a few decades ago. During the era when balls didn't hook very much and weight blocks were much lighter, drilling a ball with positive weight produced a major impact on its characteristics. While it is still a factor, it now plays a minor role in comparison to the cover material, pin placement, and positioning and type of the weight block and core.

Top and Bottom Weight

You can also change what's known as top or bottom weight. The half with the holes is the top half. If the center of gravity is toward the top half, that's known as top weight. It is designed to get your ball farther down the lane before the break

Imagine two golfers playing a round, one using the legal maximum of fourteen clubs in his bag and the other using only a five-iron for every shot. This is analogous to the difference between the bowling ball options available during my 1965 rookie campaign and the myriad options available today.

The evolution of our sport during the last thirty years is truly amazing. Only the outer dimensions have stayed the same. From synthetic lanes to proactive and reactive two-piece balls with dynamic cores to modern pins, bowling in the twenty-first century bears little resemblance to the game I grew up playing as a boy. All of these advancements have contributed to rising scores. The first big change during my career came in 1976, when Brunswick introduced the LT-48 rubber ball. It hooked much more than anything else on the market. There were some PBA events in which all sixteen match play qualifiers threw it. The stock rose for many straight shooters as they were now able to cover some boards, while my shots began hooking that much more and, physically, I had to throw harder.

Four years later AMF marketed the first urethane ball. The Angle easily out-hooked the LT-48. In the mid-1980s Excalibur came out with the first reactive-resin balls, which out-hooked regular urethane. Reactive-resin balls then dominated bowling and the shots took on a skid-snap pattern. The balance of ball power again changed after Brunswick introduced the first proactive ball in the mid-1990s. Its selling point is the ability to hook through the oil harder. It has given my shots a much more even arc, much like in my younger days.

Whenever equipment changes, some players' performance improves; others become less competitive. All of us must learn to make some physical and strategic adjustments in order to keep up. The players who have open minds and solid techniques are the best candidates to make a quicker and smoother transition.

The more you can do with ball choice, the less the lane conditions factor into your scores. I can't count the number of times I've given a lesson and been told by an amateur that his or her preferred shot is through the second arrow. I try to explain that one's shot should be dictated by oil patterns, and so it shouldn't always go over the same track. For instance, in golf I prefer to aim my drives for the center of the fairway. However, if there is a fifty mile-per-hour crosswind, a shot lofted down the middle will end up in the woods. You have to make adjustments according to the ever-changing conditions. When you see your preferred shot skidding and missing the pocket, you had better find a different strike line. Your choice of ball and strike line are critical factors. Although ball innovations over the years have effected a revolution, there was one moment that the PBA Tour changed dramatically—when the PBA hired a lane maintenance director in 1971. Prior to that it was up to each player to figure out the characteristics of each pair in each house. Ray Bluth, for example, kept a diary on every lane he rolled on throughout the entire country. But now, each PBA lane director brings a unique philosophy on how oil patterns ought to be applied. This means that we touring pros have to match our games to the director's philosophy. Certain styles fit better than others.

While great bowlers are great bowlers, most everybody has strengths and weaknesses. In my opinion, the only player who is one hundred percent versatile on every condition is Norm Duke. The other top bowlers can change their games to some degree. When conditions dictate, Parker can turn it up as much as Jason Couch. However, he will have a lot of trouble trying to beat Jason when Jason is bowling his normal game and Parker is being forced to emulate Jason's style. Conversely, Jason will come out second best when he must play Parker's game. The key is to make money with your B-game and go to town whenever the conditions are in your favor.

point occurs. Bottom weight has the opposite effect by fostering an earlier break point. Either way, no more than a three-ounce variance is legal.

Finger and Thumb Weight
Up to one ounce of variance between finger weight versus thumb weight is allowed. Place your ball so that the holes face you with the finger holes on top and the thumb hole on the bottom. Now draw a horizontal equatorlike line that goes between the finger holes and thumb hole around the center of the ball. Regulations allow up to one ounce of variance of weight toward the fingers or the thumb. Finger weight refers to the half containing the finger holes while thumb weight refers to the half with the thumb hole. Finger weight has a similar effect to positive side weight while thumb weight is akin to negative side weight. To ensure exact measurements, many of today's finer pro shops feature state-of-the-art computerized scales.

Pitch
In our sport, pitch refers to the angle at which the holes are drilled. Aside from the very important consideration of providing you with the most comfortable possible grip, pitch can be utilized to alter the characteristics of your shots.

To see what kind of thumb pitch your ball has, insert your hand into the ball and hold it out in front of you. If your thumb is positioned close to the fingertips that means the ball has forward pitch. The effect of forward pitch would be to keep your thumb in the hole for as long as possible. If instead your thumb is positioned far away from the palm in a more open position, you're experiencing reverse pitch. Reverse pitch is designed to get your thumb out of the ball as early as is feasible. Zero pitch would be the

more natural position that's between these two extremes.

There are also lateral pitches. The bending of the thumb toward the palm is known as right-handed pitch for a right-handed player and left-handed pitch for a left-handed player. This will also keep the thumb inside the ball slightly longer. Angling the thumb away from the palm affords a quicker release.

Now slightly clinch your hand as if about to make a fist. The pronounced bending of your knuckles so that the fingers are bent toward your palm is known as finger forward pitch. It will cause your two fingers to stay in the ball longer, resulting in a more pronounced hit on your release that, in turn, is designed to maximize your shot's hooking and carrying power. Reverse pitch, the bending backward of the fingers, will get the ball to leave your fingers early. It is utilized to minimize hook.

You might think that it would be good to have your strike ball drilled to increase its hook and power, while having your spare ball configured in the opposite way. However, whatever slight benefit might be gained by changing your grip's specifications would be more than offset by the resulting difference in the feel of the two balls. Remember, the key to good bowling is your ability to duplicate a series of movements shot after shot. Consistency of repetition is far less difficult to obtain if every one of your balls feels the same in your hand.

There are many factors that will help your pro shop proprietor decide what types of pitches will best serve your needs. Your hand size and the natural movement of your fingers are the most important aspects for drilling a ball. However, bowling style and body type also are taken into consideration.

HAVE BOTH YOUR SPARE AND STRIKE BALLS DRILLED WITH ROUGHLY THE SAME SPECIFICATIONS IN ORDER TO MAINTAIN A NEAR-IDENTICAL FEEL FOR BOTH.

RIGHT: DRILLING CAN SUBSTANTIALLY CHANGE THE WEIGHT DISTRIBUTION INSIDE A BALL.

Balls can even have extra holes—the legal maximum is in fact six holes total. For instance, pros Mark Williams and Sandra Jo Shiery have balls with an extra hole into which the pinky finger is inserted, which improves lift. A hole into which no finger is inserted can be drilled as a counterbalance. This is often required to keep your ball within legal limits when it has been drilled off label in an effort to introduce positive/negative, thumb/finger, or top/bottom weight to obtain the most advantageous weight block, core, and pin placement for your needs. The counterbalance hole can also change your shot's break point.

All of these drilling details can become overwhelming; don't worry about gaining a complete understanding of them. Instead become an educated consumer by speaking to some of the better bowlers you know to find out who drills their equipment. Word of mouth should lead you to a pro shop operator who knows what he or she is doing. An ill-fitting ball will not only hamper your ability to perform, it can also cause an injury. I have seen far too many bowlers who suffer severe burn marks on their fingertips and the inside of their thumbs, as well as unnecessary calluses.

PROPER ATTIRE FOR YOUR BALL

After your ball is drilled, you'll want to make sure it's properly outfitted for your needs. Tape, grips, and a wrist device will ensure a snug fit with your hand. The right shoes and bag will also make a difference in keeping your game in shape.

Tape
Every serious player should bring electrical tape, white athletic tape, or special thumb- and finger-hole tape to the lanes. Because your fingers and thumb can swell or shrink during competition or in reaction to the weather, the holes that fit like a glove when they were drilled might not always be so comfortable. Your knowledgeable pro will drill your ball so that the holes fit your hand. Should your hand swell, remove tape. If no tape

remains and the fit is still too tight, take your ball back to your pro to have the holes opened up. When your hand isn't swollen, tape can be inserted to restore that desired snug feel.

You will notice that one end of the tape is square while the opposite side is rounded. The latter is meant to be at the top of the hole. When inserting tape into the thumb hole, place it so that it rubs against your thumb without irritating the skin. A right-handed bowler should insert tape between six and eight o'clock, while a left-handed player should place tape between the four and six o'clock positions. The only time you would do otherwise is when extremely dry or cold

weather is causing the ball to slip off your thumb. In these situations, add but one piece to the front of the hole.

Similarly, the tape is placed into the finger holes to make contact with just the back of your fingers on fingernail side. The lone exception occurs when gripping the ball is extremely problematic due to the climate. In that situation, place but one piece of tape into the front of the hole to make contact with the pad of your digit. Using more than one piece would cause an alteration of your span. Although the change might be minute, it can adversely affect your ability to execute a clean release.

- USE TAPE TO GET THE RIGHT FIT WITH YOUR FINGERS AND THUMB
- USE FINGER AND THUMB GRIPS INSERTS TO ADD LIFT TO YOUR SHOTS
- USE WRIST DEVICES TO REINFORCE THE CUPPED POSITION
- BUY SHOES CUSTOMIZED TO YOUR RIGHT-HANDED OR LEFT-HANDED PREFERENCE
- USE A BOWLING BAG THAT PRESERVES YOUR EQUIPMENT

ABOVE: ONE OF ONLY A HANDFUL TO HAVE BOWLED A TELEVISED PERFECT GAME, STEVE JAROS APPRECIATES THE IMPORTANCE OF MATCHING THE OPTIMUM BALL TYPE WITH A GIVEN LANE CONDITION.

ALWAYS REMOVE A WRIST DEVICE WHEN TRYING TO MAKE A SPARE OR SPLIT STRAIGHT SHOT.

If you use finger grips, occasionally strips of tape may be placed between the grip and the inside of the hole. Thus, the fingers and thumb will make contact still only with the grip itself. When removing tape take care not to damage your grips. Using scissors or tweezers usually makes the process easier. I recommend applying rubbing alcohol on the tape so as to dampen its glue before removing it.

Finger and Thumb Grips

Grips can help you execute a smooth release consistently. To obtain a comfortable feel, consider the benefits of either finger grips or a thumb insert. These are especially useful for players who use a fingertip or semifingertip grip of the ball. Finger grips come in various sizes, shapes, and textures. Their purpose is to

Wrist Devices

In addition to grips and inserts, you can improve your strike shot's carrying power by cupping your wrist throughout the armswing, much as Steve Hoskins and Michelle Feldman do. Doing so increases the time gap between the exit of the thumb and of the fingers. The result is a more pronounced hook and, in most instances, greater carrying power. However, a cupped wrist position can place a lot of stress on a very fragile part of your body, and, unless practiced frequently, it can cause irregular shots. If you experience this problem, the solution could be to wear a wrist device.

These handy items are designed to keep your wrist locked into one position throughout your entire delivery. That position could be bent slightly backward

keep your middle and ring fingers in the ball longer. This allows you to achieve greater lift on your strike ball. Usually, you can expect to obtain at least ten percent more lift with grips than without. This occurs because your fingers are still inside the ball at the bottom of the downswing as your thumb is departing the ball. The fingers exit only after they have begun to move upward. This results in a powerful roll. The greatest argument for using thumb inserts is that they promote consistency from ball to ball for those of you who own more than one ball. The larger your arsenal, the more important this becomes. You want every ball to feel the same on your hand for whenever you must make a switch to a different strike ball or your spare ball.

(to make your shot go as straight as possible) or flat or cupped (to maximize hook). Some of the more elaborate wrist devices are adjustable. Others are designed to maintain one specific wrist position. Most are made with either metal or a sturdy plastic.

Wrist devices—especially those that promote the cupped position—are very good for newer players and for those who lack strength. Most women and many men will find them to be of great help. They're also useful for those who possess extraordinary strength (even in bowling there can be too much of a good thing). Those models that are meant to augment your hook should be removed when trying to convert a spare or a split, in which accuracy, not power, is what's required.

ABOVE LEFT: THE HEEL AND SOLE OF THIS TYPE OF DESIGN ARE REMOVABLE AND CAN BE INTERCHANGED WITH OTHER HEELS AND SOLES TO ADJUST THE AMOUNT OF SLIDE THAT THE BOWLER GENERATES. *ABOVE RIGHT*: A CURRENT SHOE DESIGN FROM DEXTER.

Thanks to modern technology, I have been cloned. As a result, there is another bowler out there who can throw shot after shot after shot exactly like me. His name is Throbot and he's also a Brunswick pro.

There are a few differences, however. I'm around six feet tall and thin; he's ten feet tall and tips the scales at roughly sixteen hundred pounds. Whereas it took me nearly thirty years to become proficient, Throbot's very first delivery was a strike, and he never rolls a 160 game under pressure. Throbot quite literally is a striking machine.

The world's most proficient bowler was conceived in America and created in Germany so that Brunswick's R&D staff could scientifically test bowling balls. Company literature describes the robot as the "industry's first precision mechanical release simulator for bowling balls." In fact, Throbot can be programmed so that its shots simulate those of any player, including yours truly. Among the variables it can accommodate are ball speed, revs (revolutions), side roll, axis tilt, and loft. Like Walter Ray, it can play any angle on the lane. Unlike Walter Ray or myself, it never gets tired or has an off day. Plus, it's available 24 hours a day and 365 days a year.

How Throbot's shots perform on any specific condition is measured by a device known as Super CATS (computer-aided tracking system). With twenty-four sensors, it scientifically plots the ball's position within one-tenth of an inch over the entire lane. Throbot's job is to test out all the ball prototypes Brunswick produces, to decide which go to market and which go back to the drawing board.

In the old days, the R&D folks designed a new ball that they hoped would give them a leg up on

their many rivals. The prototypes were produced and those of us on the pro staff became bowling guinea pigs. Our feedback was solicited regarding the quality (or lack thereof) of the new balls. In many cases, it was back to the drawing board for some fine-tuning with the cover stock and/or the weight block. While our feedback was of value, all company decisions were based on our opinions and not on fact.

First conceived in 1995, Throbot was seen as a way to improve upon measuring ball reaction from a primitive ball launcher that had been developed by the Bayer Company in their lab in Leverkusen, Germany. Bayer had long been Brunswick's supplier of polyurethane, and Bayer's best brains, under the direction of Dr. Wolfgang Jacobsen, were put to work to design and construct a tenpins robot. Dr. Jacobsen worked closely with Bill Wasserberger, Brunswick's R&D director, as well as with former PBA player and R&D expert Ray Edwards. Construction began in March 1998 and was completed five months later. No less than nine different German companies provided supplies for Throbot. Among the robot's components: a vacuum pump, hydraulic motor, pneumatic brake, digital angle encoder, a pneumatic cylinder, and suction cups. In September the fully assembled robot was flown to the States from Germany in the belly of a 747 and subsequently trucked from Chicago to its current home at Brunswick's headquarters in Muskegon, Michigan. The public unveiling came in June 1999.

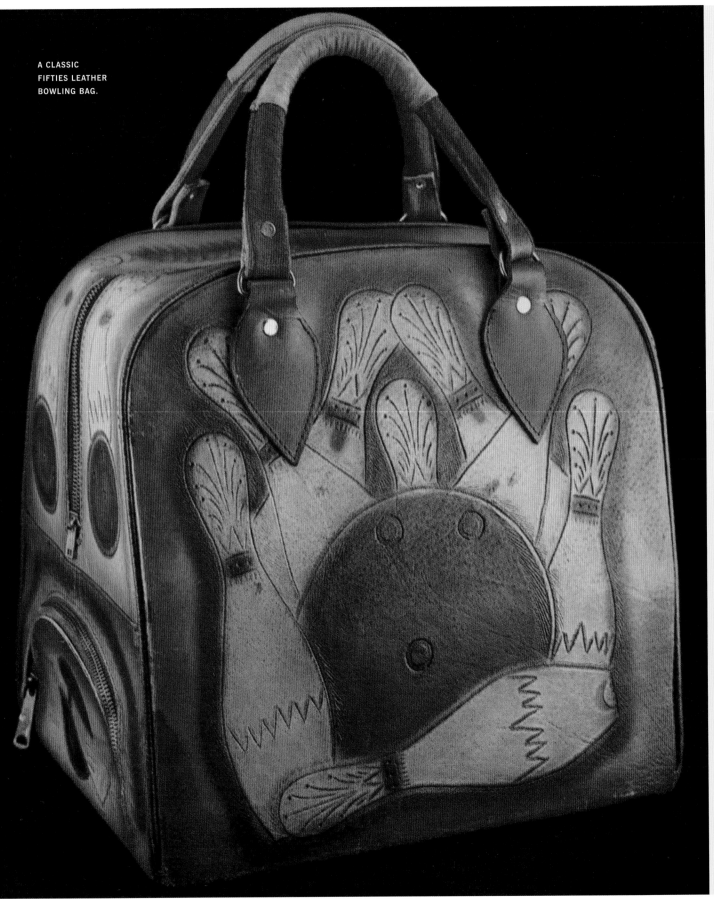

A CLASSIC
FIFTIES LEATHER
BOWLING BAG.

Once again, I suggest consulting your local pro as to which device best suits your needs and budget. Plan on spending from ten to fifty dollars.

Bowling Shoes
While finger grips, thumb inserts, and wrist devices are optional, every serious bowler should own his or her own bowling shoes. Reason number 1: economics. By the tenth time you have rented shoes you have spent enough to have purchased a pair. Reason number 2: hygeine. I'm a generous guy who likes to share, but there's something inherently unappealing about sticking my feet into shoes that have been worn by dozens of strangers. Reason number 3: performance. You will bowl better with your own shoes, especially after you have grown accustomed to them.

Few bowling neophytes realize that bowling shoes come in right-handed and left-handed varieties. In contrast, rental shoes are meant to be ambidextrous: the bottoms of each shoe usually consist of buckskin leather or suede so they will smoothly slide on the approach. Except for the very cheapest pairs, the shoes sold in the pro shop feature a slippery bottom surface only on the shoe for your sliding leg. The pivot foot's surface is likely to be rippled rubber that's designed to maximize that foot's ability to grip the floor. The greater leverage obtained translates to better balance and to being able to produce a more powerful shot.

Wearing the wrong shoes can be hazardous to your health and, in the case of one noted public figure, to your political standing as well. While making a campaign appearance on behalf of President Reagan in 1983, George Bush stopped by Milwaukee's Serb Hall Lanes. Mr. Bush was handed a pair of right-handed shoes before delivering a shot. Although his political leanings might have been slightly to the right of center, as an athlete he's a lefty. As he released his shot, Mr. Bush's right foot gripped the lane and he went flying over the foul line face-first. His unfortunate experience was captured by a photographer and subsequently published by newspapers from coast to coast.

If you just want to save a few bucks and avoid sharing germs, you can drop as little as twenty dollars. At the opposite end of the spectrum are state-of-the-art shoes that allow the wearer to change the bottoms of the sliding shoe from a very slippery surface (Teflon), which combats a sticky approach, to a rubber bottom, which is for a slick approach. You can also adjust the pivot foot's surface. For that level of luxury, expect to fork over up to $150.

Bowling Bags
To keep your shoes and your ball in the best condition, use a bowling bag that fits your needs. The old-fashioned single-ball model is fine if you only own one ball, as long as it has a separate area for your accessories and your shoes. Don't compromise by getting the cheapest bag if it means your shoes will be crushed when stored. It just doesn't make economic sense to save a few cents on your bag only to have to buy a new pair of shoes the following year after this year's pair was destroyed under the weight of your ball at the bottom of a cheap bag.

Double-ball bags currently lead the market in sales. Almost all of these have several compartments for your various items. Many also have shoulder straps and/or wheels with a retractable handle, like the better luggage seen in airports now. There are also three-ball bags as well as four-ball models, which can be separated to form a pair of two-ball carriers. The type and quality of the product means that you can spend as little as ten dollars or more than ten times that amount.

ABOVE: RENTAL SHOES AT BOWLING CENTERS ARE HARDLY EVER CUSTOMIZED FOR RIGHT- OR LEFT-HANDERS. INSTEAD, THE BOTTOMS OF THE SHOES IN EVERY PAIR ARE THE SAME, WHICH MEANS THAT YOUR FOOTWORK WILL NOT BE VERY PRECISE.

3

CHAPTER THREE: GAINING THE MENTAL EDGE

T he further you progress in bowling, the more important your mental game will become. I have observed so many players who possessed outstanding physical potential fall short of fulfilling their expectations because of their psychological limitations. While it's important for you to have good technique, proper equipment, and a fit body, it's my conviction that a poor psychological framework has significantly stymied more players than have shortcomings in all these other areas combined.

I challenge anyone to survey a list of the all-time PBA or PWBA leaders and find any player who didn't possess outstanding powers of concentration coupled with a great knowledge of bowling's intricacies. Conversely, I can name literally dozens of prospects who had trouble on the pro tours though they had every bit as much physical talent as their successful counterparts did. What differentiates success from failure is most often temperament: a sense of responsibility, discipline, and dedication.

CONSISTENT CONCENTRATION

In my opinion, every competitive bowler should do all he or she can to fully focus on each shot thrown, whether it's for a tenth-frame strike to win a tournament, a fill ball at the end of a league game whose outcome is already decided, or a shot during a Tuesday morning practice session in a near-empty center. I strive to bring just as high a level of determination and concentration to my warm-up shots as I do to those that "count." On the other hand, when a major tournament and tens of thousands of dollars are on the line for a single shot I try to be just as composed as if I were delivering a warm-up ball.

My practice philosophy is never to confuse quantity for quality. Too many players roll a large number of practice shots and convince themselves that they're working hard. But if your concentration has lagged, the reality is that you're hardly working at all. I will practice only for as long as I'm able to put one hundred percent concentration and effort into every shot. When your focus is gone your execution will be sloppy and the practice can actually be counterproductive. The only thing you're doing is practicing how to bowl poorly.

Even when a match is out of the wood, that tenth-frame fill ball is still significant. A five-person team in league play that averages a nine-count gains a ten-pin edge per game and thirty pins in total wood over opponents who typically leave three sticks standing. I can't begin to tell you how many tournaments have seen me make a cut or make the show with a one- or a two-pin margin during a forty-two game event. I know that I have gained a great advantage over pros who get sloppy on their final shot.

The best example of someone who makes the most of every shot is Mike Aulby. His ability to concentrate fully is fantastic—and it doesn't change, whether he is leading a tournament or is out of contention. I'm convinced that that is a key ingredient in his greatness as a player.

Even during the last shot of the last game of a round your full concentration remains warranted, even though the game may already be decided, because every delivery has the potential to teach you something that you can apply in the future. Having said that, there are times when I'll risk donating a pin or two on a fill shot. Let's say that the lanes are in transition (or about to enter that phase) in terms of the oil on the surface. After a lot of play the oil is beginning to dissipate and migrate, but I'm not sure exactly how much or where. The strike line, ball speed, and the ball I'm currently using might not be the best choices a game or two later in the tournament. In that situation I will make an educated guess as to how the lane conditions will evolve and what I will need to use to conquer the new conditions. I will then try out my new estimation with perhaps a new strike line, ball speed, or ball. Thus I might glean some valuable information toward formulating a new plan for the fully transitioned lanes.

I also recommend concentrating when your fill ball provides you with an easy-to-convert single-pin spare. Let's say you're a right-handed player who has left the 2-pin (or you're a lefty faced with the 3-pin). A piece of cake, right? But who is to say that your next delivery might not see you faced with having to cover the bucket (2-4-5-8 for a righty or a 3-5-6-9 for a lefty)? By having given one hundred percent on the single-pin leave you can determine where the ball has struck the pin. This will allow you to determine what adjustment, if any, will be needed when you're faced with the bucket. There is but one topic that should consume your thought process on the lanes: What will I do on my next delivery so as to produce the best shot I possibly can?

SHUTTING OUT DISTRACTION

I have often heard Mike Aulby declare that when he is in a "zone" he is so focused on his game that he wouldn't notice if a bomb exploded behind him.

- TREAT PRACTICE AND TOURNAMENT SHOTS WITH THE SAME LEVEL OF CONCENTRATION

- DO NOT CONTINUE TO ROLL PRACTICE SHOTS IF YOU HAVE LOST YOUR CONCENTRATION

- EACH SHOT HAS THE POTENTIAL TO TEACH YOU SOMETHING NEW

- USE SIMPLE SPARE CONVERSION SHOTS AS AN OPPORTUNITY TO TEST LANE CONDITIONS

Perhaps the greatest example of great performance under pressure came when Johnny Petraglia produced the first eleven strikes on national television during the championship round of the 1994 PBA National Championship. Having edged Eric Forkel in the opening game of the TV finals, Johnny had to challenge reigning Player of the Year and all-time great Walter Ray Williams Jr. Much was on the line to the eventual winner, including one of men's pro bowling's three major titles, a $27,000 payday, and a three-year exemption into the Brunswick World Tournament of Champions.

Johnny got off to a great start while Williams struggled (Walter ended up with a 194). Burying shot after shot into the one-two pocket, my fellow New Jersey left-hander entered the tenth frame with nothing but X's to the right of his name. Shots ten and eleven were every bit as perfect as their predecessors.

Ducat's Imperial Lanes became so quiet that one would have thought that Toledo had been abandoned. The fans knew they might be witnessing history, as Johnny was attempting to duplicate a feat that had happened on only six occasions in the more than thirty years ABC-TV had been airing PBA events.

Johnny steadied himself just as he had done when he needed a strike to win one of his fourteen career titles. Now, a generation after his best year, the wizened warrior was grasping for one more moment of bowling fame. He went through his preshot routine just as he would if he were practicing. He moved forward toward the foul line, his delivery concluding with the great deep knee bend that is his trademark. As millions of viewers held their breath, Johnny's ball inched toward the pins. Seeming to take an eternity to arrive, it finally reached its destination.

Yes, it was right in the pocket, but we all know that's no guarantee of success. After all, many a great player has ever so slightly squeezed his fingers upon releasing a key shot, and that infinitesimal difference is just enough to allow a ball to deflect slightly and leave a corner pin standing. Any bowling fan over forty vividly recalls the image of Don Johnson lying on his stomach after the last shot of the 1970 Tournament of Champions left a solid 10-pin to deprive him of perfection during the title game of our sport's ultimate event (his consolation was a 299–268 win over Dick Ritger in what many experts have labeled the greatest game ever bowled). Unlike Johnson, Petraglia saw ten sticks disappear.

It's at moments like these when one draws upon any prior experience that will aid one's confidence. All of us on tour go through periods when our level of self-belief is sky-high. There are also times when it hits rock bottom. Johnny's zenith came in 1971, when he defeated Don Johnson in the championship game of the Tournament of Champions. That was the final of a PBA record-equaling three consecutive tournaments that he won to conclude the winter tour. He captured five events that year and edged out Johnson for the earnings crown with his career-best of $85,065. When I was a young player under Johnny's wing, he once told me that never in his life has he felt as confident as he did in 1971. I asked him what he was thinking that year before he had to make a key shot. His response: "I knew that I had struck and now I just had to let go of the ball so that everyone else would know it too!"

Can you imagine having to roll one ball with so much at stake? Most people would be unable to function. What separates a Johnny Petraglia from the average competitor isn't that he feels any less nervous. Rather, it's that he has had to roll countless do-or-die shots and has learned how to best function when so challenged. Once again, I

recommend that after a pressure situation you spend a few moments reviewing how you fared and why. Literally make note of what occurred. Periodic review of such data should reveal a pattern. In turn, this will help you to devise a plan that will help you to excel the next time you are feeling apprehensive.

Perhaps that's a bit of an exaggeration but it does make an important point. It is all too easy to become unsettled by the actions of players on adjacent lanes or by inconsiderate people who make noise just as you're delivering a shot. However, becoming perturbed will do you no good. Neither will becoming angry when Lady Luck appears to play favorites to someone else's advantage. Such is the nature of bowling—you could roll a seemingly good shot but fail to carry, while a foe goes through the beak and strikes.

Many times what appears to be luck isn't quite as fortuitous as one might think. If you're taking on Walter Ray Williams Jr. you know that he will trip a lot of 4-pins, owing to his entry angle into the pocket and the way his ball rolls. However, he isn't nearly as likely to carry a light hit as a power player like Bob Learn Jr. or Jason Couch would be. Whether or not an opponent's good fortune is due to particular skill or luck, I know, in advance, that it is inevitable that there will be times when I will out-bowl an opponent and lose. I also know that there will be occasions when someone out-bowls me and I will win. Over the long haul luck will tend to even out. The reality is that there is no defense in bowling. You can control only your own destiny and not that of anyone else. I'm convinced that it is pure folly to focus on anything other than what you need to do on your next shot. Your challenge is to not allow an opponent's good fortune to play on your mind.

As with folks in your league, pros run the emotional gamut. Aulby and I are noted for our even-keeled personalities. A spectator who wandered into the center in the middle of the game could never ascertain from Mike's expressions or body language if he was red-hot or ice-cold. Nor am I into theatrics. If things aren't going my way I don't feel that I have the right to act like a petulant child, thereby potentially distracting my fellow competitors while stealing the spotlight from those who deserve it by virtue of doing well. Moreover, getting mad doesn't make you bowl better. I have even been criticized for being too calm. Hall of Famer Marshall Holman, now an analyst for ESPN, says that I would do better if I were more like him. But he will also concede that he lost some tournaments when he became overly emotional.

Another common distraction is, ironically, the scoreboard. A few open frames render us overly frustrated or angry, and the consequence is an inability to perform. Conversely, a string of strikes gets us so excited that we start working out mathematical equations ("three more in a row for a 250 . . ."). Now the adrenaline is pumping and we run to the line as if we were Carl Lewis. Different circumstance, same result: an inability to perform. The solution: don't bowl against an overhead TV screen. Bowl against the pins!

Just as a baseball player can't hit a six-run homer, you can't produce a six-bagger on a single shot. Whether or not you've just opened or are on a string of strikes, you can roll only one strike on your next delivery. How to do so must be your focus.

Sometimes it's best to take a defensive strategy. One hallmark of great players and teams is that they very rarely beat themselves. Don't bury yourself by failing to fill frame after frame. If you've just suffered back-to-back splits the smart play might be to select safety: focus on hitting the pocket without imparting a few thousand revs (revolutions). Get a nine-count, cover your spare, and slowly regain your confidence. Always grind out a decent score that's within ten to fifteen pins of your average. By averting Titanic-like games you put yourself in a great position to win tournaments.

However, despite all these warnings against distractions, you do need to pay attention to the environment in which you're competing—without becoming distracted by it. While bowling on tour I am acutely aware of the scoring pace. It's of little use to average 210 for a block when the field is at 240. On the other hand, a 220 is a great game when the field

- DON'T LET GOOD OR BAD LUCK DISTRACT YOU
- DON'T LET YOUR EMOTIONS TAKE CONTROL
- DON'T FIXATE ON THE SCOREBOARD—BOWL AGAINST THE PINS
- DON'T BEAT YOURSELF UP OVER A POOR STRETCH
- DO PAY ATTENTION TO THE GENERAL SCORING ENVIRONMENT

ACHIEVING CONSISTENCY OF PERFORMANCE IS GREATLY AIDED BY ESTABLISHING AND FOLLOWING A CONSISTENT PRESHOT ROUTINE.

• MASTER PRESSURE BY TURNING IT INTO A TOOL FOR BETTER PERFORMANCE

• ANTICIPATE YOUR TENDENCIES UNDER PRESSURE AND COMPENSATE FOR THEM

• FOCUS ON WHAT CAN BE IMPROVED, NOT WHAT HAS GONE WRONG

is at 215. The trick is to get the most out of every pair of lanes that the conditions and my abilities will allow. In any endeavor, athletic or otherwise, consistency is a secret to success.

PRESSURE

No matter how often I'm in a title game, there will always be the proverbial butterflies in my stomach. None of us is impervious to pressure. The trick is how you handle bowling while subjected to duress. First, consider your perspective. Do not become distracted by pondering the potential rewards of success or the consequences of failure. Remind yourself that pressure is nothing more than a reward for having performed well. After all, I wouldn't be feeling any pressure if I needed a strike to finish thirty-seventh. There's only pressure if I have put myself in a position where I have a chance to win. The proper attitude is to remind yourself of how well you have been faring so far, to enhance your level of confidence.

Of course, staying calm on a key shot is easier said than done. Clearly, the ideal is to perform exactly the same on a pressure shot as you had on the ones that preceded it. If you can, more power to you. A deep breath after stepping onto the approach helps. Release it slowly. Remind yourself of your preshot routine and then focus on your target. Then make the best shot that you possibly can.

Most of us, myself included, have regular tendencies in such situations. Jason Couch often hits harder on his release so his shot will hook more. Thus, Jason likes to give his key shot an extra board or two of room. Ryan Shafer has been known to pull up slightly at the line. He counters that by moving his target a board or two closer to the pocket while getting his ball farther down the lane. In my case, I get an adrenaline rush. I remind myself of the great shots I've made with positive self-talk and visualization. I then take a deep breath on the approach to help keep me as calm as possible. Even with that, I am quite likely to

get a bit fast with my feet and to throw the ball a little bit faster. My form of compensation is to look slightly to the inside (right) of my target. The trick is not necessarily to try to keep from becoming tense, but to be able to perform while you are tense.

I work hard at having a positive outlook prior to executing each shot. I'm convinced that self-doubt leads to self-destruction. Once I have settled upon a strategy for my upcoming shot it's vital that I do not deviate. Never doubt or second-guess yourself. The bowler who asks himself, "Can I do this?" has set himself up for failure. Tell yourself: "I can do this." Positive thoughts beget positive results. Negative thoughts become a self-fulfilling prophecy.

Being a perfectionist is an admirable trait. But those of you who are highly motivated will also experience the pitfalls that come with lofty ambitions. I was competing in a PBA Regional Tour event and crossing with a prominent touring pro who began a game with five straight strikes.

The last time that I checked, one can't do better than to have struck on every shot. That obvious fact notwithstanding, he was miserable. On his first shot he'd wandered slightly high and had to trip the 4-pin. That was followed by a messenger hit that eliminated the 10-pin a split second before the rack descended. Next came slapping out the 10-pin on a half-hit. Two other less-than-optimum strikes followed.

After each shot he came back shaking his head while eyeing his shoes. Not surprisingly, the sourpuss's game soon went south. He suffered a pocket 7-10 in the sixth frame. Even so, he had 146 pins in the bank at that juncture, which means he was on pace for a 226 and would have shot in the 240s at the rate he was going (with the opportunity to strike out for a 266). Even at our level, those are pretty good numbers. Instead, he proceeded to miss the pocket the next four frames on a pair of lanes where he had put his first six shots close enough to have struck. The

PBA STAR MARSHALL
HOLMAN IS KNOWN
FOR EXTREME DISPLAYS
OF EMOTION DURING
COMPETITIONS.

- USE POSITIVE
  VISUALIZATION BEFORE
  AND DURING PLAY

- ENGAGE IN POSITIVE
  SELF-TALK

- DEVELOP A CONSISTENT
  PRESHOT ROUTINE
  WITH PSYCHOLOGICAL
  SIGNIFICANCE

ABOVE: ERIC FORKEL'S
WORK HABITS AND
EVEN-KEELED DISPO-
SITION HAVE BEEN
KEY FACTORS IN MAK-
ING HIM ONE OF
THE PBA'S STEADIEST
PERFORMERS.

result: a sub-200 game.

The player of whom I'm writing has done okay for himself on the tour, but he's never made it into the elite despite having the requisite talent to do so. His ability to beat himself up mentally has placed a needless stumbling block into his path that he has yet to hurdle.

Understand, too, that not every bowler in the history of the sport always executes up to expectations. Whether you are Earl Anthony or a once-a-month moonlight participant, there will inevitably be some shots that you wish you had back. Whenever you toss a split, miss the pocket, or squander an easy spare it is essential that you analyze what went wrong so as to be able to implement a correction for the next time you're in a similar situation.

Once the analysis has been completed it's time to focus on positive thoughts. Never dwell on a bad shot. Always remember that while one bad shot can dig a hole, becoming angry or flustered will dig your grave.

MENTAL DEVICES

One mental device that is becoming increasingly prevalent among top-level players is that of visualization. Quite literally, before an important frame I have closed my eyes and pictured myself in action while delivering a shot that rolls over my target before crashing into the pocket and sending all ten pins disappearing into the pit.

Another trick is to engage in positive self-talk. One of the nation's finest collegiate programs is that of Wichita State University. Long-time coach Gordon Vadakin is a strong proponent of stressing the mental game. Before a season commences he asks his players to analyze where their game is and where they want it to be by the year's conclusion. They write down their goals.

Coupled with that are WSU affirmations: "I always make great shots," "I make every spare," "I fill every frame." The players are expected to repeat these phrases to themselves several times every day. Yes, it sounds silly to outsiders. However, I know of many WSU alum who have reached the pro ranks who swear that such steps helped them to get to where they are today.

Mental devices come into play especially within the preshot routine—the routine that precedes every delivery. All pro bowlers have their own unique choreographed series of actions to best ready them for their subsequent shot. Any fan who has seen Mike Aulby bowl knows that he always blows into his thumb hole before inserting his fingers into his ball. Jason Couch wipes his ball with his towel prior to every shot. Kim Terrell rubs her sliding foot on the approach just before she steps onto the lane.

What might appear to be idiosyncrasies to casual observers are, in fact, rooted in functional considerations. A dry thumb hole should help to assure a smooth release. A ball that is free from excess dirt and oil will roll more truly. And a shoe that isn't impeded by any foreign substances will prevent a potentially dangerous situation in which the player's sliding foot sticks or slips at the point of release.

Develop your own individual preshot routine based on your concerns and needs. It will minimize the specific physical nuisances that may impede your delivery, and it will provide you with a psychological edge. By duplicating the same series of actions before every shot you remind yourself that, whether you're rolling a strike to win a match or practicing in an otherwise empty center, the required movements are the same.

Long before I turned pro I established my preshot routine. By engaging in an identical choreographed series of actions before every shot you are better prepared to execute a good delivery while subconsciously establishing that there is absolutely no difference in what must be done in the first frame of a practice game or when a trophy is on the line. A major contributing factor in the televised perfect game that I rolled against David Ozio in Wichita was my regimen: it helped me to forget what was at stake and to minimize my nervousness.

No two preshot routines are identical. The steps I take all have a logical benefit in helping to prepare myself. The key to your own preshot routine is that you engage in the same steps in the same order prior to every shot. This applies to the most simple of spares as well as when warming up or practicing.

Prior to stepping onto the approach I check the pins to be certain that they are properly spotted. PBA rules allow players to demand up to two reracks per game. I then wipe the bottom of my sliding shoe with a towel. I lift my ball from the rack, immediately removing any foreign substances, including lane oil, by spinning the ball against my towel. I extend my bowling hand over the air blower until my fingers are dry.

At this point, as a left-handed player, I slide my right foot onto the approach. This is a key safety precaution to ascertain that there are no foreign substances that would prevent me from sliding properly. If my foot sticks or is excessively slippery I immediately put the ball down, step off of the approach, and rectify the problem. When the slide is smooth, I lift my ball and I gently blow into the thumb hole. I have found that doing so provides a more comfortable feel, especially given that I use ample tape. With the ball cradled against my chest, I place the inside of my right

foot on the appropriate board and then step with my left foot into my stance. As a matter of personal preference, I use a four-step delivery, with my left foot starting slightly farther back from the foul line than my right. A five-step left-handed player could position the left foot a few inches closer to the foul line than the right.

Supporting the ball with my right arm, I insert the fingers of my left hand. After they become comfortable, my thumb enters the ball. I hand the ball outward and upward before gradually lowering it to waist height. My bowling arm's elbow is now tucked into my side. The ball's deliberate descent is accompanied by my eyes finding my target. I take a deep breath and gradually exhale to relax my body.

In 1992 I began working with a sports psychologist. She incorporated verbal self-reminders into my routine. Before every shot I tell myself, "Heel, toe; heel, toe." By stepping on my heels during each of my first three strides before the rest of my shoe touches the approach, my weight stays back to provide better leverage and balance. Next I tell myself, "Palm up and open." This is to make certain that my thumb doesn't prematurely pivot. After getting set on the approach, I say to myself, "Watch the target all the way through until the ball rolls by it." Concentrating on my eyes staying focused greatly improves the accuracy of my shots.

Should anything distracting occur during your preshot routine I suggest you put your ball down and step off the approach. Only after fully gathering your thoughts and regaining composure are you ready to bowl. At that point, start your routine all over again.

CHAPTER FOUR: BUILDING YOUR SHOT

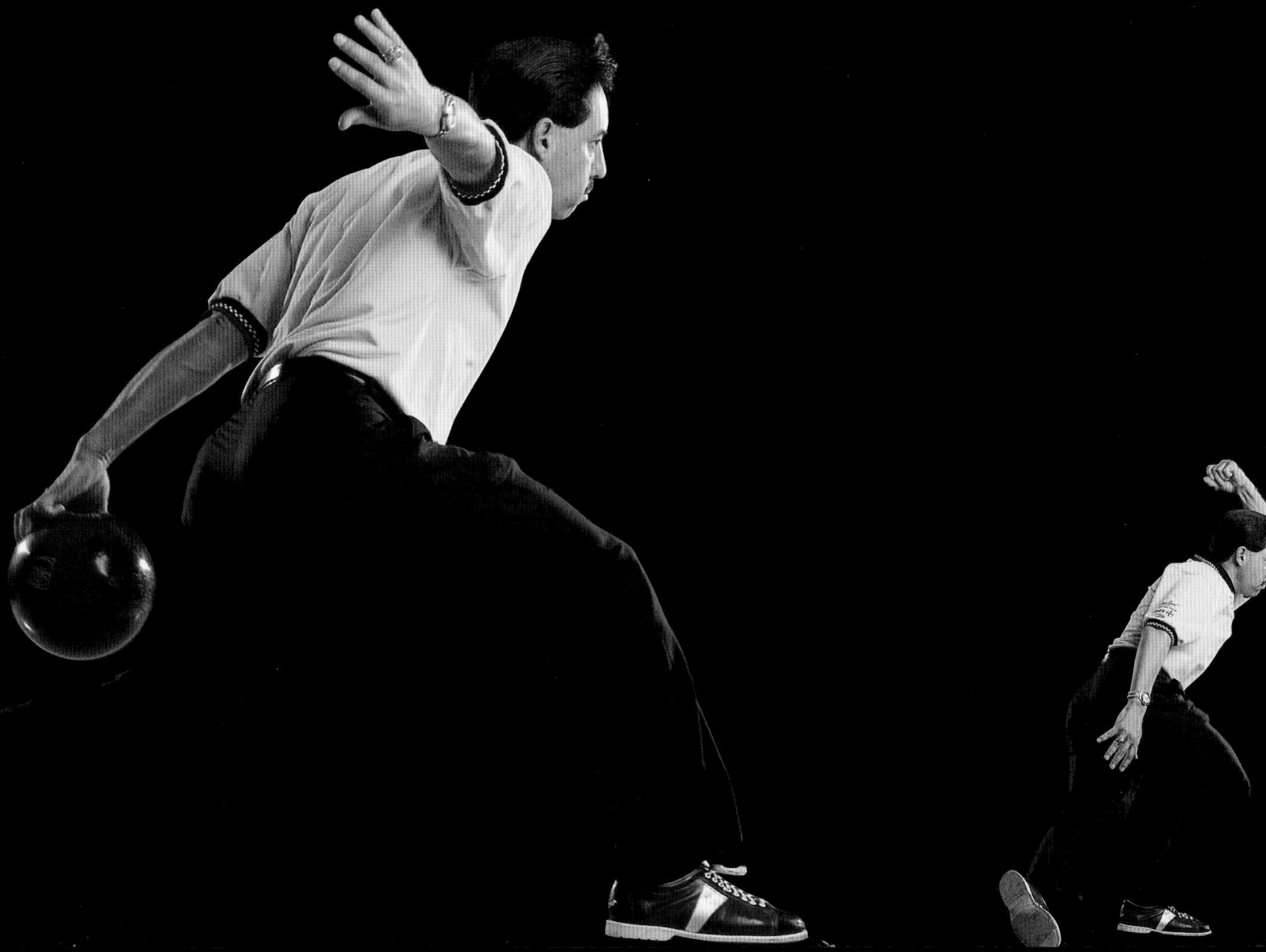

T here is a popular aphorism that declares that "what counts in bowling isn't how, it's how many." We've all seen very successful players who thrive despite idiosyncrasies in their deliveries. They are able to overcome an apparent "flaw" because of their ability to duplicate the same series of motions shot after shot.

Former ABC-TV expert commentator Nelson Burton Jr. often likened Amleto Monacelli's arm-swing and release to someone starting a lawnmower. I'd probably shatter my arm if I ever attempted to duplicate Amleto, but back-to-back Player of the Year recognitions starting in 1989 prove that it works for him.

When I first hit the tour I bowled against Ted Hannahs. He stood all the way to the right on the approach, with his footwork drifting so dramatically that he actually released the ball at the middle of the foul line. Ted frequently quipped that he would be the world champ if everyone were forced to bowl like him. Although I would never recommend that you bowl like Ted, he did win three times on the national tour.

While there is not one clear right way to get to the foul line, all of the elite players that I have observed feature the same common critical components at the point of release for both their spare shots and strike shots:

- The bowling hand is either under or slightly to the side of the ball, with the palm side of the fingers facing toward the pins;
- The shoulders and hips are parallel to the foul line, with the sliding foot pointed directly forward;
- The eyes are riveted on the target;
- The player is fully balanced;
- The ball is projected onto the lane, with the fingers exiting on a plane that is in front of the sliding foot, with the ball traveling near that ankle for maximum leverage;
- A full follow-through is executed.

How you get to the point of the release is up to you, but in general it is far easier to consistently hit a target with a straight armswing than with one that's circuitous.

The more basic and simple your movements, the easier they are to repeat. This is especially evident for bowlers who don't have the luxury of practicing or competing daily. It is with this principle in mind that the components of bowling's critical skills are analyzed (see pages 88–97).

While keeping in mind that nothing is etched in stone, I do believe that you will probably experience greater success by trying my suggestions. On the other hand, don't fix what isn't broken. If you are content with your current results there is no reason to correct a "mistake" if it isn't impeding your ability to repeat.

THE BASIC HOOK STRIKE SHOT

Step one: knock over all of the pins. Beginner bowlers might want to start out with a straight shot for their strikes, but the hook shot is always a better bet because it packs more power. With either a straight or hook shot, your target pins will be the same.

Pin Hits

Believe it or not, during the "ideal" strike shot your ball actually makes contact with only four of the pins. A right-handed player's shot enters the 1-3 pocket, which sets off two simultaneous chain reactions: the 1-pin hits the 2-pin that hits the 4-pin that hits the 7-pin, while the 3-pin takes out the 6-pin that then eliminates the 10-pin. Meanwhile, the ball pushes the 5-pin into the 8-pin before the ball knocks over the 9-pin. A left-hander's shot enters the 1-2 pocket with the ball nudging the 5-pin into the 9-pin. The ball then rolls over the 8-pin. The headpin sends the 3-pin into the 6-pin with the 6-pin taking out the 10-pin. At the same time the 2-pin propels the 4-pin into the 7-pin. Ideally, all of the pins end up in the pit.

Should your ball deflect after contacting the headpin—that is, veer off to one side from its intended course through the center pins—the likely result will see a corner pin left standing. Leaving the soft 10-pin (for a righty) or 7-pin (lefty) isn't due to bad luck. Rather, your shot was light or deflected so much that the 6-pin (righty) or 4-pin (lefty) fell lazily into the gutter instead of taking out the corner pin. A ringing 10-pin or 7-pin occurs when the 6-pin or 4-pin is sent upwards and barely flies around the outside of the corner pin's neck. Often, that corner pin will just be nudged out long after the other pins have been eliminated. You know that you have imparted a good release to your shot if you see that pin fall inwards.

In order for this to occur, sufficient inertia must exist so that the ball heads straight through all the pins on its track. Without this inertia, there will be deflection—when the ball hits the first pin or two and veers off to one side instead of smashing through the intended targets. A shot lacking power and/or being slightly "light" (impacting more against the 2- or 3-pin than the headpin) will cause the 2-pin (lefty) or 3-pin (righty) to fly backward rather than sideways. In turn, the 4-

- THE HOOK SHOT IS YOUR BEST BET AT MAKING A STRIKE

- THE IDEAL STRIKE SHOT SHOULD MAKE CONTACT WITH ONLY FOUR CENTRAL PINS

- USE BALL CHOICE, GRIP, WRIST POSITION, AND HAND ROTATION TO GIVE YOUR SHOT HOOK

- THE HOOK SHOT SHOULD FOLLOW A SKID-ROLL-HOOK PATTERN ON THE LANE

- CHOOSE THE DELIVERY METHOD—FOUR- OR FIVE-STEP—THAT WORKS BEST FOR YOU

- FOR THE GREATEST ACCURACY MAINTAIN A PENDULUM ARMSWING WITH DISENGAGED MUSCLES

- FOR SYNCHRONIZED TIMING YOUR FINGERS SHOULD EXIT THE BALL AS IT REACHES THE FOUL LINE

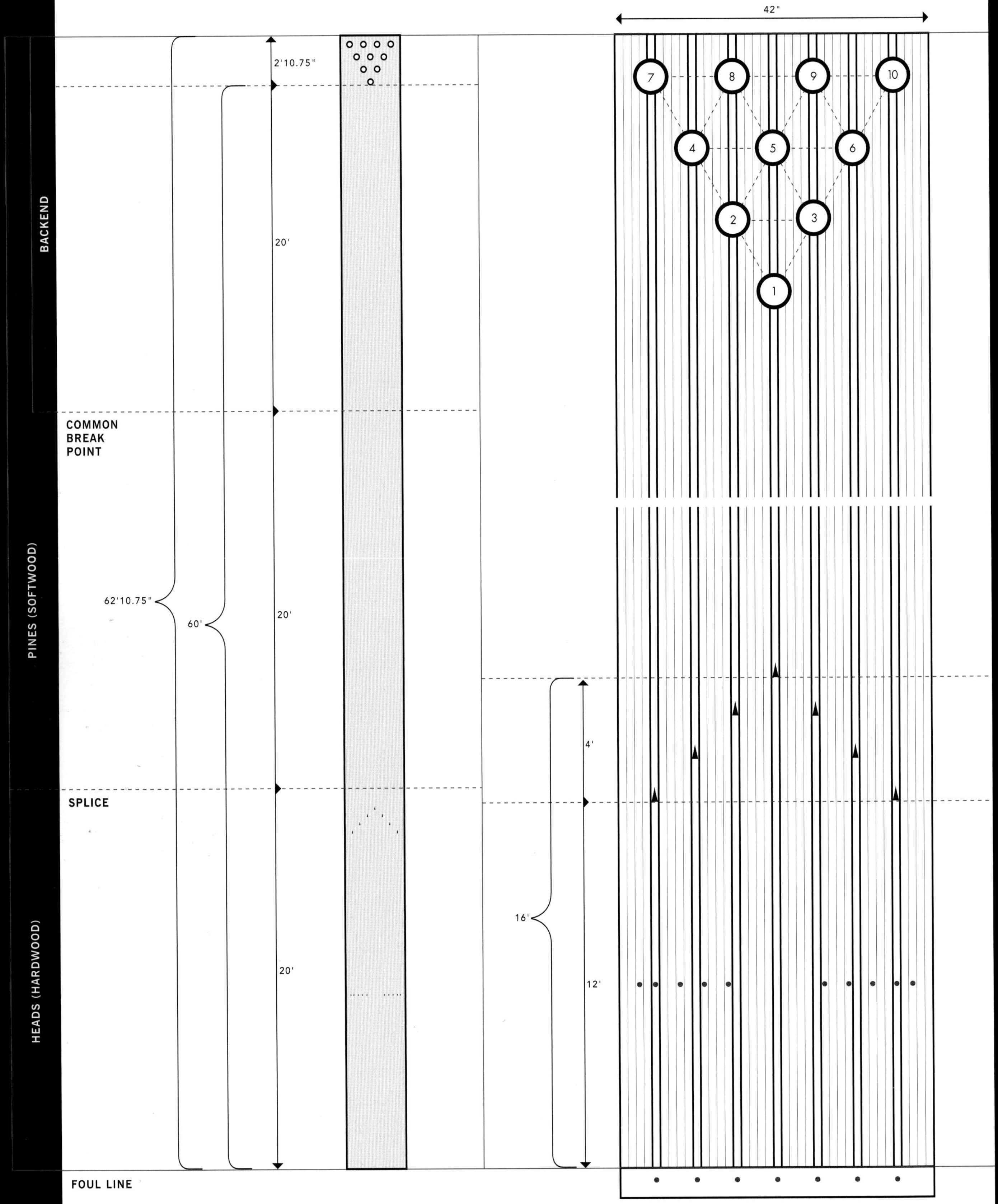

BACKEND

PINES (SOFTWOOD)

HEADS (HARDWOOD)

COMMON
BREAK
POINT

SPLICE

FOUL LINE

2'10.75"

20'

62'10.75"

60'

20'

20'

42"

7   8   9   10

4   5   6

2   3

1

4'

16'

12'

pin (lefty) or 6-pin (righty) goes in front of the respective corner pin, which leaves the bowler facing a 7-pin (lefty) or 10-pin (righty). If deflection is even more acute and/or the shot is very light, the 5-pin could be left standing, as well. So-called deflection splits include the 5-7 and 8-10 for a right-handed player and the 5-10 and 7-9 for left-handers.

On the other hand, excessive power can hinder your ability to strike. A ball that overpowers the headpin will continue hooking and drive straight into the center of the 5-pin, instead of more to the side of the 5-pin. As a result, the 8-pin (lefty) or 9-pin (righty) fails to fall.

While we've outlined the standard strike scenario, there are in fact several ways that your strike shot can knock over all the pins. One alternative strike is called the wall shot; carry occurs after a light hit when the ball is finishing strongly. Initially, the 2-4-5 (for a right-hander) or the 3-5-6 (left-hander) are standing. They are wiped out as the headpin ricochets off the far sidewall and comes back into play. Another strike shot, the messenger hit, involves the headpin flying off the left sidewall to take out the 10-pin (for a righty) or off of the right sidewall to eliminate the 7-pin (lefty). Sometimes, a shot that is slightly high will carry. The trip-four (righty) or trip-six (lefty) also involves some help from the far sidewall. A right-hander's shot sees the 2-pin hit off that wall before taking out either the 4-pin or the 4-7 combo. A left-hander's shot relies upon the 3-pin to do the damage on the 6-pin or on the 6-10.

While it is possible for you to use a straight shot to strike, your better bet will always be a shot that hooks. The hook shot gives you a greater margin for error because it has greater power. Some amateurs even roll a backup ball that curves to the right for a right-handed player or to the left for a left-handed player. Both the backup and straight shot lack enough power to allow you to consistently strike. I don't know of any pros or even high-level amateurs who roll their shots in such a manner. That's why I strongly rec-

ommend that you hook the ball on your strike shots unless you are a younger or lower-average player who is still striving to achieve a modicum of accuracy. Any player who can average 150 or above is capable of learning how to throw a hook ball for strike shots.

How to Hook

There are several ways to make your shot hook, or curve, as it approaches the pins. Your choice of equipment, grip, wrist position, and hand rotation all can help impart hook on the ball. The surface and interior weight distribution of your bowling ball vary widely to either minimize or maximize the hooking action (see chapter two for more on ball composition). A conventional grip means that your middle and ring fingers are inserted into the ball fully up to the second knuckle. It is generally utilized by beginners and younger players. It will aid accuracy but retard hook. Conversely, a fingertip grip (in which those two fingers enter the ball only up to the first knuckles) or semifingertip grip (in which the fingers enter up to between the first and second knuckles) will cause your fingers to remain in the ball well after your thumb during your release. The result is increased lift, and, with it, ball rotation. Another way to produce hook is the cupped wrist. (On the other hand, bending the wrist backward is utilized in an attempt to get the ball to roll straight.) Finally, rotating the hand clockwise (lefty) or counterclockwise (righty) just before the release will impart spin that leads to a hooking motion.

The Skid-Roll-Hook Pattern

Your strike shot has three phases. The "heads" portion of the lane (the front segment of the lane nearest to the foul line, which on a wooden lane consists of hard maple) is protected from the impact of bowling balls by a coating of lane conditioner—that is, oil. Your ball will skid through this part of the lane and will revolve only a few times, at most. Just past the arrows, the maple gives way to

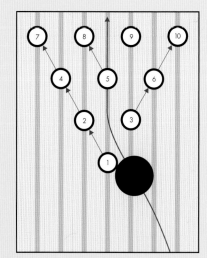

RIGHT-HANDER'S IDEAL POCKET HIT AND PIN CARRY

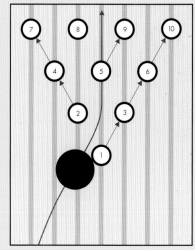

LEFT-HANDER'S IDEAL POCKET HIT AND PIN CARRY

SKID-ROLL-HOOK PATTERN

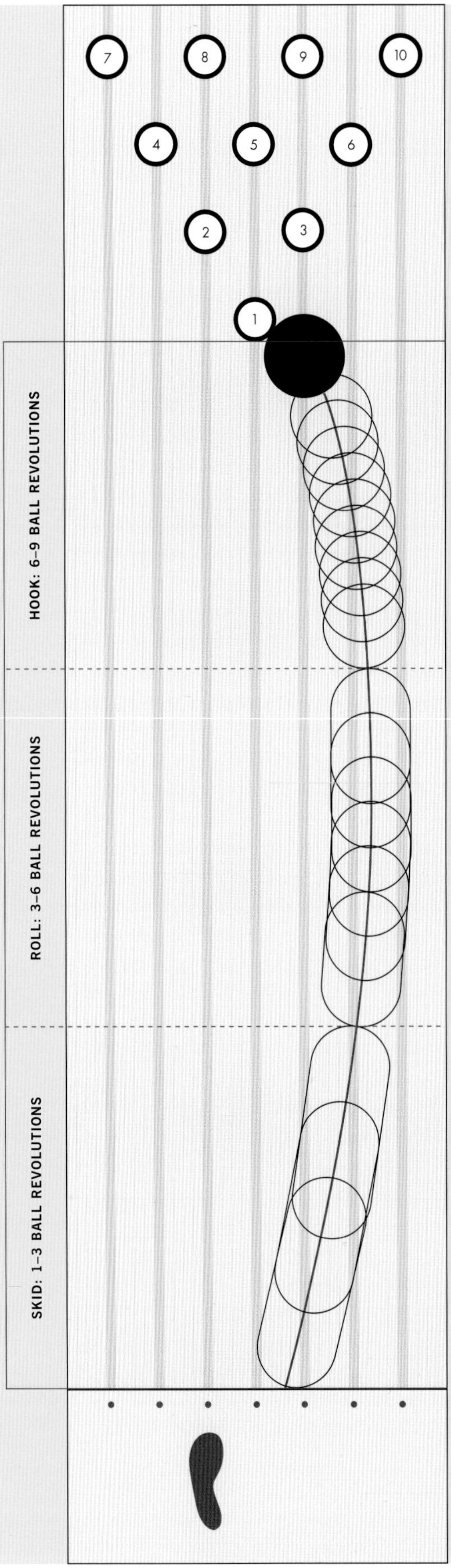

HOOK: 6–9 BALL REVOLUTIONS

ROLL: 3–6 BALL REVOLUTIONS

SKID: 1–3 BALL REVOLUTIONS

pine. This part of the lane is known as the splice. By this midpoint of your journey your ball will start to roll on what is called the midlane.

Finally, as it enters the drier rear third of the lane (better known as the backend) a hook ball will change its trajectory. In many cases, players who impart significant power to their shots will be able to notice the ball producing far more revolutions at this point (this is known in bowling parlance as having your shot "rev up"). At this point your ball has acquired greater inertia that will minimize deflection when it hits the pocket. Even on a synthetic surface, the skid-roll-hook pattern will prevail.

On most lane conditions, it is advantageous to save the lion's share of your ball's energy for the moment it contacts the pins. However, as noted above, excessive inertia can result in overpowering the pins. If you are faced with a lot of taps of the 8-pin (lefty) or 9-pin (righty), it may be better for your shot to actually "roll out." This phenomenon occurs when your shot's hooking arc decreases or concludes as it approaches the pins. Amleto Monacelli is the master of this technique and he's almost unbeatable when lane conditions demand such a shot. For an advanced player, the secret to achieving a controlled rollout is to turn the ball fairly extremely during your release to increase the amount that the ball turns over on the lane, especially while in the midlane.

The Four- or Five-Step Delivery
Whether you're making a hook shot strike or a straight shot to convert a spare, you will need to follow a consistent sequence of motions to get you to the point of the ball's release. The best way to order and synchronize these motions is with a set number of steps. Virtually every player of quality uses a four- or five-step delivery that concludes by sliding on the foot that is opposite to the bowling hand. There is but one difference between the four- and five-step players. The latter generally take a very

short initial shuffle step with the foot opposite from their bowling hand. That step precedes any movement of the bowling ball. From that point onwards, the two kinds of delivery are identical. You should take your initial stance at whatever distance makes sense for you. Of course a four-step bowler will begin closer to the foul line than a five-step bowler. The easiest way to figure your distance is to walk back from the foul line toward the approach with four or five and a half steps, depending on the kind of delivery you prefer. The half step is to account for your slide.

The next movement for the five-step player and the initial step for the four-step bowler sees the right foot (for a righty) moving forward. As that occurs, the ball is handed out in a straight line off your shoulder and toward your target. This motion, the pushaway, coincides with the heel of your foot's touching the approach. The next step sees the ball moving backward. The following stride (third step for a four-step player and fourth step for a five-step bowler) coincides with the top of the backswing. During the final step the knee opposite the bowling arm bends and your body is gradually lowered with your swing coming down to your side and the ball adjacent to the ankle of your sliding foot. The ball is released just as the sliding foot slides to the foul line. This is known as synchronized timing. Players wishing to add power at the possible expense of some accuracy will employ late timing (see page 91). They plant the "sliding" foot as the downswing is proceeding so as to obtain greater leverage.

Many experts believe that it is better for beginners to start with the four-step delivery because it is simpler. After a player gains experience and improves, synchronizing foot and hand movements should become less problematic. At that point, the four- or five-step question is merely an issue of individual preference.

The Free Armswing

Whether you use a four- or five-step delivery, your delivery should be married to what's known as a pendulum armswing. To visualize this concept, picture a ball on the end of a string that is attached to a fulcrum. In this case, your shoulder is the fulcrum and your arm is the string. Ideally, the ball will swing your arm and not the other way around. Thus, we bowlers hope to engage as little of our arm's muscles as possible during the armswing.

The more "free" is your armswing, the less likely it is to veer off course. By allowing your arm to swing in a straight line you should be far more accurate. All that you need to do is to hold the ball in line with the outside of your shoulder during your stance. Hand it directly forward during your pushaway, and allow it to swing in a natural straight manner throughout the delivery. Conversely, players who "wrap" the ball behind their back or "bump" it well away from their body during their delivery are using their muscles to guide the ball. Combined with the circuitous movement of their arm, it is very difficult for them to achieve consistency.

The free armswing also allows you to alter your shot's speed easily. Greater speed makes the ball hook less, and less speed makes the ball hook more. The higher that you hold the ball during your stance, the farther back your ball will reach behind you in the backswing, and the longer the whole armswing will be. This will increase your speed. Holding the ball below waist height will decrease speed.

The Release

A "clean" release in which your thumb and, subsequently, your fingers smoothly exit from the ball will help your ball to land on the lane beyond the foul line much like an airplane lands on a runway. The exit of the fingers occurs just as your hand passes by the ankle of your sliding foot so that the ball is projected forward and slightly upward. A common flaw among lower-average players is to lay the ball short by releasing it as the armswing

WHEN MISSING INSIDE OF YOUR TARGET, FOCUS ON STAYING DOWN WITH THE SHOT WHILE INTENTLY WATCHING YOUR BALL ROLL OVER YOUR TARGET (TO AVOID PULLING UP YOUR BACK).

1. & 2. TO DECREASE
THE LENGTH OF YOUR
ARMSWING IN ORDER
TO DECREASE BALL
SPEED, HOLD THE BALL
LOWER (BELOW WAIST
HEIGHT) DURING YOUR
STARTING STANCE.

3. & 4. FOR NORMAL
BALL SPEED, I START
HOLDING THE BALL AT
WAIST HEIGHT.

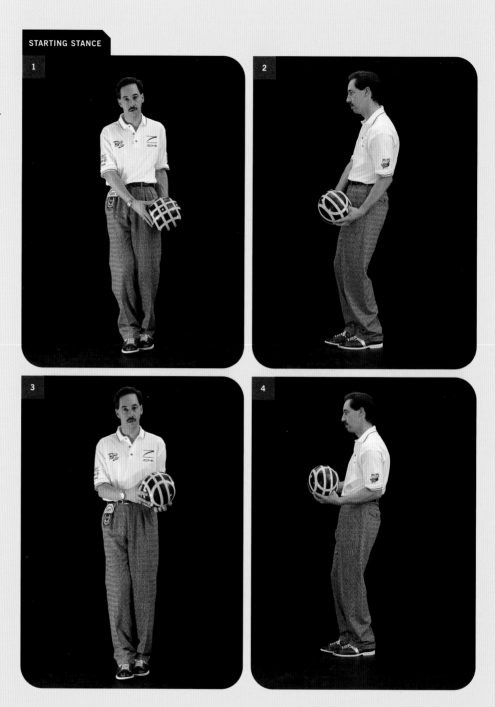

STARTING STANCE

STARTING STANCE

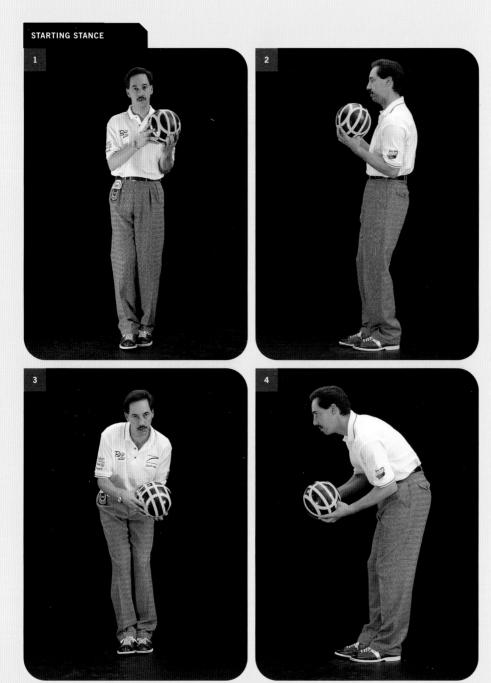

1. & 2. TO INCREASE THE LENGTH OF YOUR ARMSWING IN ORDER TO THROW THE BALL FASTER, HOLD THE BALL HIGHER (ABOVE WAIST HEIGHT) DURING YOUR STARTING STANCE.

3. & 4. NO MATTER WHAT HEIGHT THE BALL IS HELD, DON'T HUNCH OVER AT THE WAIST.

1. & 2. A PUSHAWAY
THAT PRECEDES FOOT
MOVEMENT WILL CAUSE
YOU TO BE EARLY
IN YOUR TIMING AND
MAY COMPROMISE
YOUR BALANCE.

3. & 4. I RECOMMEND
THAT YOUR PUSHAWAY
BE SYNCHRONIZED
WITH YOUR STRIDE
FORWARD WITH YOUR
NONSLIDING FOOT.

is still on its downward trajectory. This will cost you leverage and, with it, decrease power.

There are certain lane conditions that call for projecting the ball farther out onto the lane. Known as lofting, this sees your ball landing three to six feet beyond the foul line. This strategy is used to combat hooking (dry) heads so that your ball doesn't needlessly expend its finite amount of energy prematurely. However, when lofting your shots it is essential that the ball is propelled forward rather than upward. Lofting is achieved by giving the ball a slight outward lift just before releasing the ball.

THE STARTING STANCE

- Check the adjacent lanes for clearance; then remove the ball from the rack and step onto the approach.
- Slide your sliding foot on the approach to make sure no sticky items are on the bottom of that shoe.
- Set your feet on the approach by lining up with the inside of your sliding foot before inserting your hand into the ball.
- The fingers enter the ball first, followed by the thumb.
- The ball is held in line with the shoulder and is at or slightly above waist height.
- To increase ball speed, hold the ball higher during the starting stance; to decrease ball speed, hold the ball lower.
- Square the entire body to the foul line.
- Remind yourself of one or two physical and/or mental keys. Take a deep breath, exhale, and begin the delivery.

Common Mistakes to Avoid
- Failure to concentrate fully on all shots, even the seemingly easy ones.
- Holding the ball to the center of the body, thus forcing the swing to loop to clear the hips, or having to walk out of the shot so the ball clears the hips.

THE PUSHAWAY

- In the starting stance the ball is aligned with the shoulder of the bowling arm.
- The ball is handed directly forward on a plane that is parallel to the ground.

- The sole of the opposite-sided foot touches the lane as it strides forward and the ball begins its descent.

Common Mistakes to Avoid
- Holding the ball in front of the torso so that the arm must swing circuitously just to clear the body.
- Dropping the ball into the swing.

THE ARMSWING

- Following the pushaway, the arm's muscles are disengaged, allowing gravity to pull the ball downward.
- The arm acts much like a string that is attached to a pendulum. By minimizing the use of the arm's muscles it is far easier to have the arm swing in a straight line.
- The length of the armswing's arc is primarily determined by the height at which the ball was held during the address. The higher the position, the greater the arc and the greater the resulting ball speed.

Common Mistakes to Avoid
- Muscling the shot.
- The swing's bumping outward from the body in the early stages, which causes the ball to loop.

SYNCHRONIZED TIMING

- The simultaneous arrival at the foul line of the sliding foot and the bowling hand is desirable to promote balance.
- The second step (of a five-step delivery) or the first step (of a four-step delivery) is made with the foot that is on the same side as the bowling hand, with the heel first touching the approach as the ball begins to fall following the pushaway.
- For a five-step delivery the first step (with the opposite foot) is usually fairly short, and the subsequent stride is longer.
- The top of the backswing coincides with the next-to-last step. As that occurs, the knee of the sliding leg is bent as the body begins its gradual descent.

Common Mistakes to Avoid
- Getting "fast" with the feet.
- Inconsistency of the pushaway, leading to being early or late with the timing.

BACKSWING

1. & 2. THE SECOND
STEP OF A FOUR-STEP
DELIVERY SEES
THE BALL BY YOUR
SIDE AS IT SWINGS
BACK BEHIND YOU.

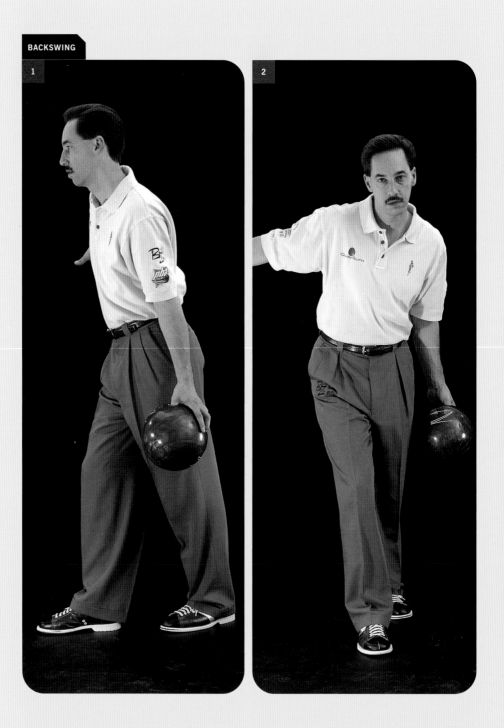

TOP OF THE BACKSWING

1. & 2. A HIGH BACK-SWING HELPS MAXIMIZE BALL SPEED. NOTE THAT IN THESE TWO PICTURES THE FEET ARE A STEP AHEAD OF THE ARMSWING—LATE TIMING, WHICH CAN SOMETIMES GIVE YOU ADDED LEVERAGE.

3. WITH NORMAL TIMING IN A FOUR-STEP DELIV-ERY, THIS IS THE THIRD STEP, ALSO KNOWN AS THE POWER STEP. THIS SHOWS A NORMAL HEIGHT BACKSWING.

LATE TIMING

- Many power players obtain added leverage at the point of release by planting their opposite foot (left foot for a right-handed bowler and right foot for a left-handed bowler) while the ball is still in the downswing.
- Movement by the sliding foot precedes the pushaway.
- The final step is primarily downward so that, after a short slide, the foot is fully planted during the release.

Common Mistakes to Avoid

- Loss of balance at the point of release by trying to overthrow the ball.

THE RELEASE

- The head remains steady throughout the entire delivery. You can help to achieve this by riveting the eyes on the target until after the ball has traveled beyond the arrows.
- The knee of the sliding leg bends as the body gradually lowers during the downswing.
- The thumb should automatically exit the ball before the fingers.
- After the thumb exits, the bowling hand rotates either slightly counterclockwise (for a right-handed player) or clockwise (left-handed player).
- A pronounced bend of the sliding leg's knee will maximize leverage and power.
- The ball is projected out onto the lane so that it lands a few feet beyond the foul line in much the same manner as an airplane lands on a runway—with a gradual forward-moving descent instead of a quick downward drop.
- Following the release the bowling hand should swing through the target in a straight line through the target to begin the follow-through.
- Throughout the delivery the opposite arm extends outward to improve balance. It may extend parallel to the floor, or more directly upward—whichever works best for your balance.

Common Mistakes to Avoid

- Dropping the ball onto the lane. During practice, place a towel just beyond the foul line and focus on projecting the ball beyond the towel.
- Having the thumb of the bowling hand pointed downward, or the palm over the ball.

FOOTWORK

- Stride with the toes facing directly forward.
- Except during the slide, the heel of each foot contacts the lane first, followed by the toes.
- Upon releasing the ball and until the follow-through is completed, the front part (the toes) of the pivot (nonsliding) foot remains in contact with the approach.

Common Mistakes to Avoid

- Drifting excessively (five or more boards) during the approach.
- Pointing the toes of the sliding foot in the direction of the bowling hand during the release (therefore not being perpendicular to the foul line), causing a loss of balance and open hips.

BALANCE

- Maintain even weight distribution in your stance.
- All strides are within shoulder width.
- The opposite arm extends to provide a counterweight.
- Make a pronounced knee bend during the pivot step, which is next to the last step, to gradually lower the body, thus allowing the sliding leg to absorb your body weight.
- The trail foot's toes slide on the approach.
- The length and arc of the armswing are proportionate to the player's strength, so the ball's weight doesn't cause a loss of balance.

Common Mistakes to Avoid

- Excessively long pushaway.
- Pulling the ball through the shot during the downswing.

WHEN MISSING WIDE DUE TO DROPPING THE SHOULDER OF YOUR BOWLING ARM, IT IS ADVISABLE TO FOCUS ON KEEPING YOUR SHOULDERS EQUIDISTANT FROM THE FLOOR DURING YOUR STARTING STANCE.

COMMON MISTAKES

1. & 2. TO AVOID BEING OFF-BALANCE DURING THE DELIVERY, REMEMBER TO USE YOUR OPPOSITE ARM (LEFT FOR RIGHT-HANDERS) AS A COUNTERWEIGHT TO THE BALL. THE BEST WAY TO DO THIS IS TO EXTEND THE OPPOSITE ARM STRAIGHT OUTWARD. CLUTCHING IT INTO THE CHEST OR RESTING IT ON YOUR KNEE, AS SHOWN HERE, WILL UPSET YOUR BALANCE.

3. WHEN YOU'RE AT THE TOP OF YOUR BACKSWING, DON'T LET THE SHOULDER OPPOSITE YOUR BOWLING ARM DROP OR TWIST DOWN; KEEP YOUR SHOULDERS SQUARE THROUGHOUT THE DELIVERY.

4. WHEN YOU RELEASE THE BALL BEFORE YOUR FOOTWORK IS FINISHED, YOUR TIMING IS EARLY—WHICH IS NEVER REALLY DESIRABLE.

1. THE CUPPED WRIST
POSITION IS USED TO
MAXIMIZE HOOK.

2. THE NORMAL (FLAT)
WRIST POSITION.

3. BREAKING THE WRIST
BACKWARD "KILLS THE
SHOT" IN ORDER TO
MAKE THE BALL ROLL AS
STRAIGHT AS POSSIBLE.

WRIST POSITIONS

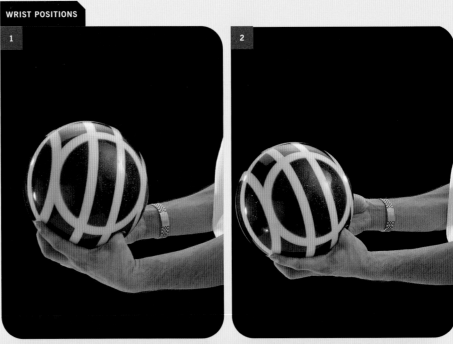

ADJUSTMENTS FOR THE BACKSWING

- High (above shoulder height)

  Advantage: Increases ball speed to help keep shot on line (on dry lanes and/or for most spares).

  Disadvantage: Possible loss of control.

  Key: Holding ball higher during address to increase arc length naturally without having to muscle shot.

- Normal (shoulder height)

  Advantage: Excellent for maximizing accuracy and control.

  Disadvantage: Insufficient ball speed on dry lanes.

  Key: Proper timing established during pushaway.

- Abbreviated (waist height)

  Advantage: Slower speed to conquer tight (oily) lanes.

  Disadvantage: Harder to keep ball on line.

  Key: Shorter and slower strides to maintain timing.

WRIST POSITIONS

- Cupped

  Advantage: Maximum revs (revolutions).

  Disadvantage: Possible sacrifice of control.

  Key: Keep bowling wrist locked throughout entire armswing.

- Normal (flat)

  Advantage: Maximum accuracy.

  Disadvantage: Fewer revs (revolutions).

  Key: Release the ball beyond the plane of the sliding foot.

- Bent backward

  Advantage: Straightest possible shot (ideal for covering most spares).

  Disadvantage: Unnatural feel for most players.

  Key: Focus on maintaining wrist position during the backswing.

BALL PROJECTION

- Lofting

  Advantage: Combats the detrimental effects of dry heads (the first fifteen feet of the lane beyond the foul line).

  Disadvantage: Tendency to pull up on the shot or to produce an inconsistent loft distance. Both of these can change your

amount of hook.

  Key: Maintain posture and balance at the point of release.

- Normal

  Advantage: Consistent roll throughout the entire shot.

  Disadvantage: Can be inappropriate as lanes change.

  Key: Consistent release of ball beyond the foul line.

- Laying short

  Advantage: Early roll overcomes heavy oil.

  Disadvantage: Disastrous when heads hook early.

  Key: Accentuate follow-through.

HAND POSITIONS

- Sideways suitcase

  Advantage: Keeps ball on line on a tight lane.

  Disadvantage: Minimal hooking action with potential for weaker finish.

  Key: Keep your hand on the ball's side throughout the entire delivery.

- Underneath grip

  Advantage: Solid on many conditions due to emphasis on accuracy.

  Disadvantage: Not sufficiently powerful to open up an oily lane.

  Key: Maintain the same hand position throughout the entire point of the release.

- Hand Rotation

  Advantage: Powerful roll with maximum backend reaction.

  Disadvantage: Possible sacrifice of accuracy and/or consistency.

  Key: Consistency of hand movement and sliding foot synchronization.

PLACING YOUR HAND MORE TO THE OUTSIDE OF THE BALL WILL HELP YOU KEEP YOUR SHOTS ON LINE.

TUCKING YOUR PINKIE FINGER BY BENDING IT TOWARD YOUR PALM WILL CREATE MORE SPIN AND THUS ADD ABOUT TWO TO THREE BOARDS OF HOOK TO YOUR SHOT.

RELEASE

1. & 2. FOR A NORMAL
AND CONTROLLED
RELEASE YOUR HAND
SHOULD LEAVE THE
BALL JUST AS IT PASSES
YOUR ANKLE.

3. HOLDING ONTO THE
BALL TOO LONG AFTER
IT HAS PASSED YOUR
ANKLE MAY RESULT IN
EXCESSIVE LOFT WITH
THE POTENTIAL FOR A
LOSS OF CONTROL.

There are some women and many men who are born with natural power that allows them to more easily create ample ball speed and revs (revolutions). If that's you, then consider yourself fortunate. Even if you aren't in that category, though, you can greatly upgrade your power. At five-feet-six and 140 pounds, I am neither among the bigger nor smaller players on the PWBA tour. To me, size isn't a major consideration. Norm Duke is one of the smallest PBA players but he can rip on the ball as well as anyone. And although very thin, Pete Weber is able to maximize his power to out-strike far more husky opponents. Power is relative. I'm not claiming that I (or any other female bowler) can hook the ball with Bob Learn Jr. or that any of us can generate anywhere near the amount of hard revs (revolutions) of Steve Hoskins. Nevertheless, a top female player can certainly create more than enough area to get the job done. There is no reason why we can't open up a lane and be able to carry halfhits.

While many men rely on muscle mass, we counter with attributes that are within our range of ability. I can keep up with far bigger and stronger women because of the leverage that I consistently produce during my release. That's attributable to a combination of timing, wrist rotation, and the force that is generated by my legs.

Incorporating impetus from your legs requires two ingredients: fitness and technique. To keep fit, I work out regularly and include strength training in my regimen. Running can help, too, but there is no substitute for spending hours on the lanes. The second aspect is to lower your body gradually by bending your knees during your power step (the step that precedes your slide). Push off with the balls of your near-sided foot (the right foot for a right-handed player) against the approach. Then slide with the opposite leg under your body to maintain balance.

During my release the ball is also underneath my torso and is adjacent to the ankle of my sliding leg. That puts me into the optimum position to have my hand remain underneath the ball before coming around it. My wrist remains cupped throughout my entire armswing so as to get more revs (revolutions) on my strike shots.

The most significant factor involves timing. I'm fractionally "late." In other words, my slide has just concluded as the ball is about to arrive at the foul line. That I am able to maintain that consistent foot-hand relationship is essential. My lift is greatly enhanced only if my timing is just right. To accomplish that, I must focus on my pushaway barely preceding the conclusion of my first full stride (the second step if you're using a five-step delivery).

The final consideration involves equipment. In many ways, ultra-powerful modern bowling balls have negated some of the disadvantages of players who lack body mass.

Although generating power is always an important attribute, it doesn't mean that a player without double-digit revs (revolutions) can't bowl well. You must simply bowl according to your natural attributes. If your physique isn't conducive to throwing a lot of balls then focus on other assets, such as accuracy. It would be a mistake to try to hit so hard on your release that your balance, timing, and leverage would be compromised.

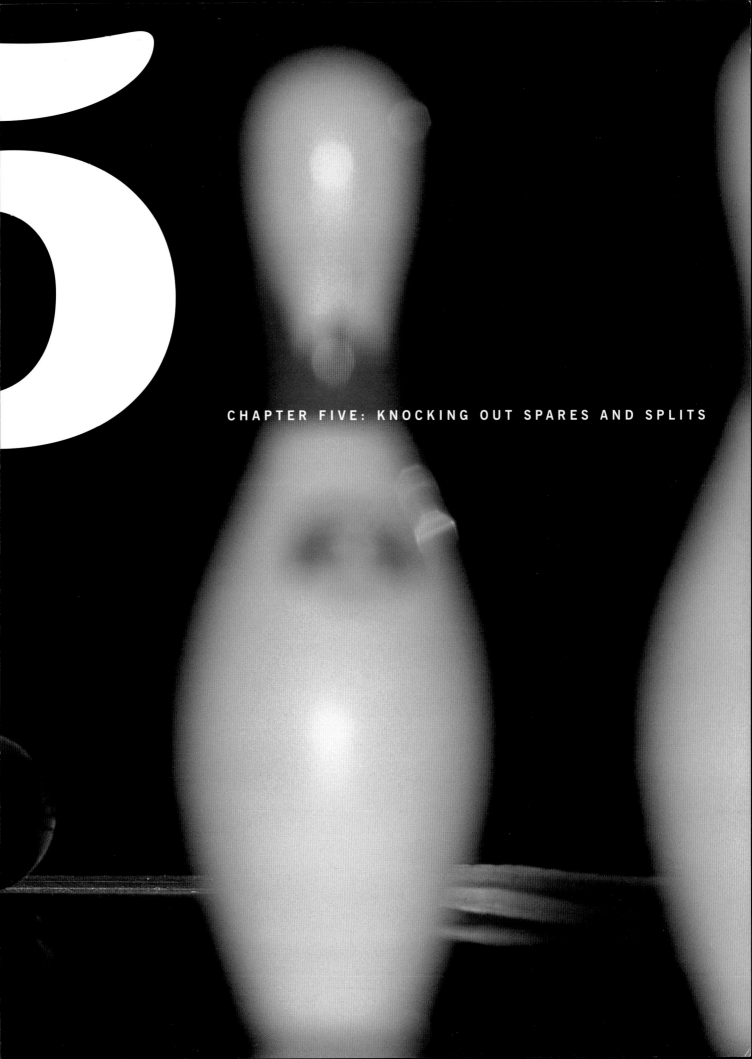

CHAPTER FIVE: KNOCKING OUT SPARES AND SPLITS

When I was a teenager I would often challenge an area pro named Charlie Delplato. The stakes were ten dollars a game, and I probably handed him a few more Alexander Hamiltons than I won. It seemed as if not one of our matches was decided before the tenth frame. If I struck I won. However, if I needed to convert a spare to win, it was, at best, a fifty-fifty proposition. I can still vividly recall being told by Charlie after losing one evening that my strike ball was far more powerful and effective than his was, but if I finally learned how to shoot spares he wouldn't be able to touch me.

Being nineteen and headstrong, I paid his advice absolutely no heed. About a year later I was still losing to Charlie while practicing to go out on the PBA tour. The great Mark Roth, a four-time Player of the Year and owner of thirty-four PBA titles (as of then only Earl Anthony had won more), had seen me bowl and told me that he was impressed by my potential. However, he added, there is one thing that you will have to improve if you're to succeed against the best players in the world. My ears perked up. Parker, he told me, you must learn how to fill frames by covering your spares.

FOUR-TIME PLAYER OF
THE YEAR MARK ROTH
IS A FIRM BELIEVER
IN THE IMPORTANCE OF
A STRONG SPARE
CONVERSION SHOT.

- THE STRAIGHT, CROSSLANE SHOT IS RECOMMENDED FOR SPARE CONVERSIONS

- INCREASE BALL SPEED BY HOLDING THE BALL HIGHER IN YOUR INITIAL STANCE

- USE A FLAT WRIST POSITION TO DECREASE BALL REVOLUTIONS, MAKING THE BALL GO STRAIGHTER

- CONSIDER USING A BALL WITH A LESS-POROUS SURFACE

- KEEP YOUR BODY PERPENDICULAR AND YOUR ARMSWING PARALLEL TO YOUR CROSSLANE TARGET

- FOR LEFT- AND RIGHT-SIDE SHOTS TRY TO USE THE SAME RESPECTIVE TARGET ARROW AND CHANGE ONLY YOUR FOOT POSITION

Up until that point most of my practice sessions had consisted of trying to roll strikes. If any pins remained standing I would push the reset button. Early on while Mark and I first practiced together I left a five-pin. Of course, there is no easier spare in bowling, so there wasn't any need for me to waste my time covering it. As I walked back he looked at me and said, "Don't touch that button. Only when you tell me that you can make one hundred out of one hundred of them do you not have to shoot it." He then added, "If you want to do well on tour you can't afford to throw any pins away."

The critical principle that you must embrace is to comprehend that in every sport there is a tradeoff between accuracy and power. The more of one that you seek to obtain, the less of the other that you will enjoy. As discussed in the last chapter, a hook shot provides more power than a straight shot. But, to hook the ball at a single-pin spare is ludicrous, as virtually no power is required to knock it over. The greater the amount of hook, the less accuracy. This is especially apparent when the oil pattern isn't consistent from gutter to gutter. You might be rolling your ball over a part of the lane that either has less or more oil than you had anticipated, therefore either accentuating or retarding the number of boards that your ball will cover.

HARD AND STRAIGHT

For most spares, I suggest that your shot be completely straight. The only exception could be the option of playing off of your strike line for certain spares, such as a double-wood combination. Even then, the mantra I prefer is: straighter is greater. Trust me, accuracy prevails over power when it comes to filling frames by converting your spare opportunities. Of course, to knock out a spare with a straight shot, you want to position yourself so that the ball will go across the lane in a straight diagonal line. This insures the best impact with the lone pin or two still standing.

To eliminate hook requires a few simple physical steps. First, hold the ball well above waist height during your address position before pushing it straight forward. This will increase the length of your armswing and, with it, ball speed. Second, keep your wrist in the flat position to decrease the gap between the thumb and finger exit, thereby eliminating several revs (revolutions). Third, keep your body square to the line throughout your delivery. Finally, keep your wrist and palm behind the ball and come straight through on your release.

You can also change equipment. If you are wearing a wrist device that is designed for strike shots and locks you into a cupped position it should be removed. You can also use a harder-surface and less-porous ball whose characteristics minimize lane-ball friction. This should retard the amount your shot will hook.

Even with all of the above, you still may not be able to go as dead straight as a Mark Roth. If that's the case, lane predictability (or the lack thereof) can become an issue. Whenever possible, the suggested formulas on the pages ahead advise you to avoid the heaviest traffic areas between the second and fourth arrow on the right side. The less-used and, thus, smoother left side of the lane tends to be more predictable. That's why it provides a better option for many spares.

With every spare that requires a straight ball, all of your movements from the pushaway to your footwork to your armswing are directed at your target; your torso is perpendicular to your target while your armswing is parallel to your target. During the follow-through drag the toes of your back (nonsliding) foot along the floor behind you and hold this position. Your eyes should remain riveted on the designated target arrow until the ball has crossed over it.

Having said all of that, keep in mind that the vast majority of players have some idiosyncrasies in their deliveries. Although I consider myself to be a fundamentally sound bowler, my spare game

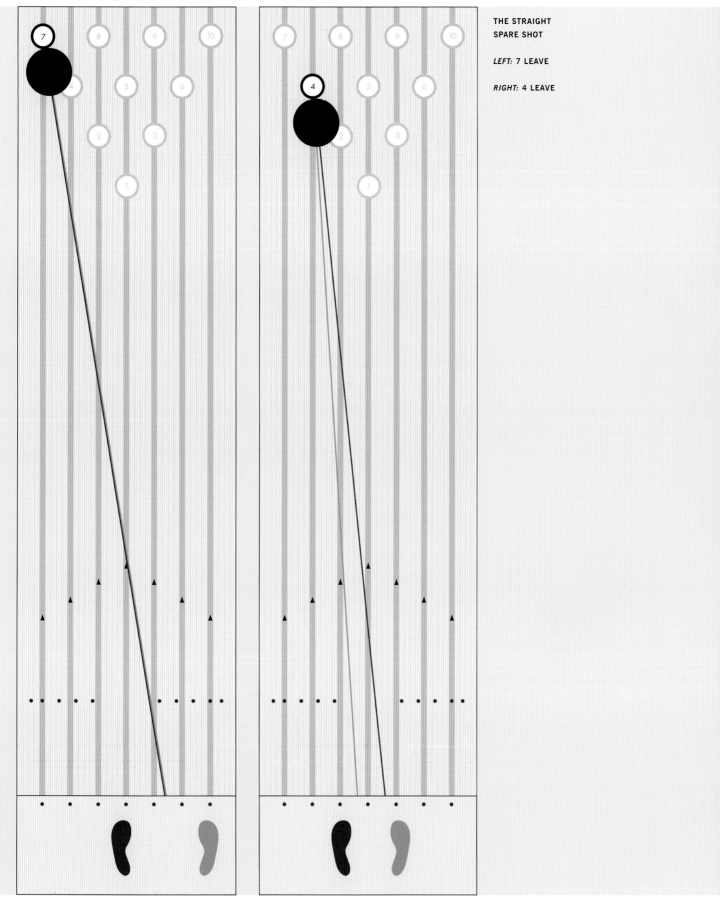

**THE STRAIGHT
SPARE SHOT**

LEFT: 7 LEAVE

RIGHT: 4 LEAVE

**THE STRAIGHT
SPARE SHOT**

LEFT: 2-7 LEAVE

RIGHT: 3-10 LEAVE

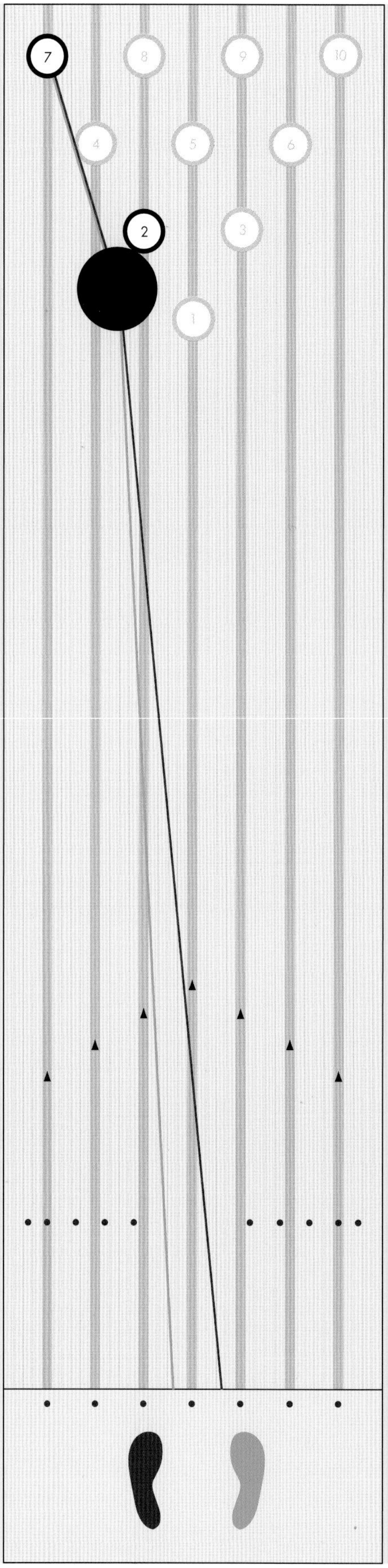

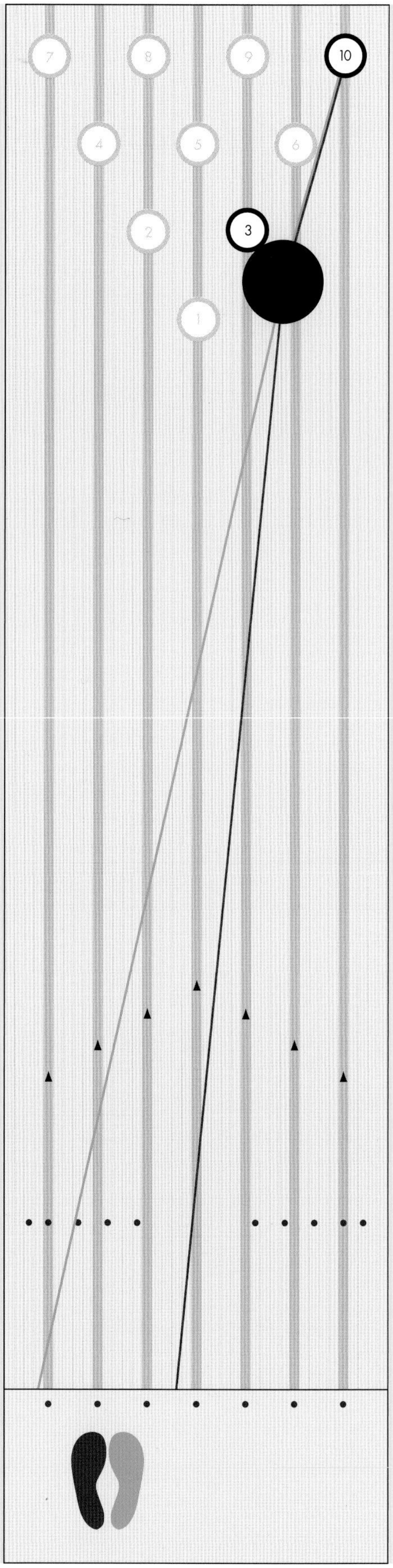

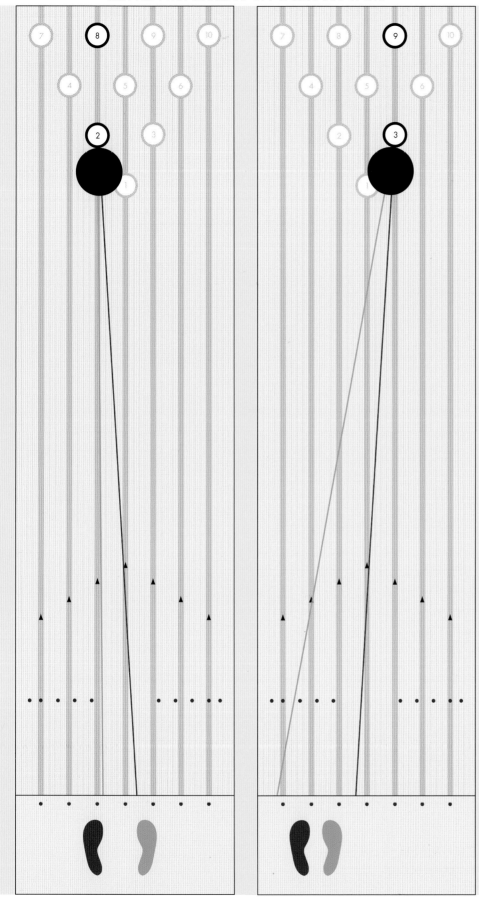

**THE STRAIGHT
SPARE SHOT**

LEFT: 2-8 LEAVE

RIGHT: 3-9 LEAVE

**THE STRAIGHT
SPARE SHOT**

LEFT: 6 LEAVE

RIGHT: 10 LEAVE

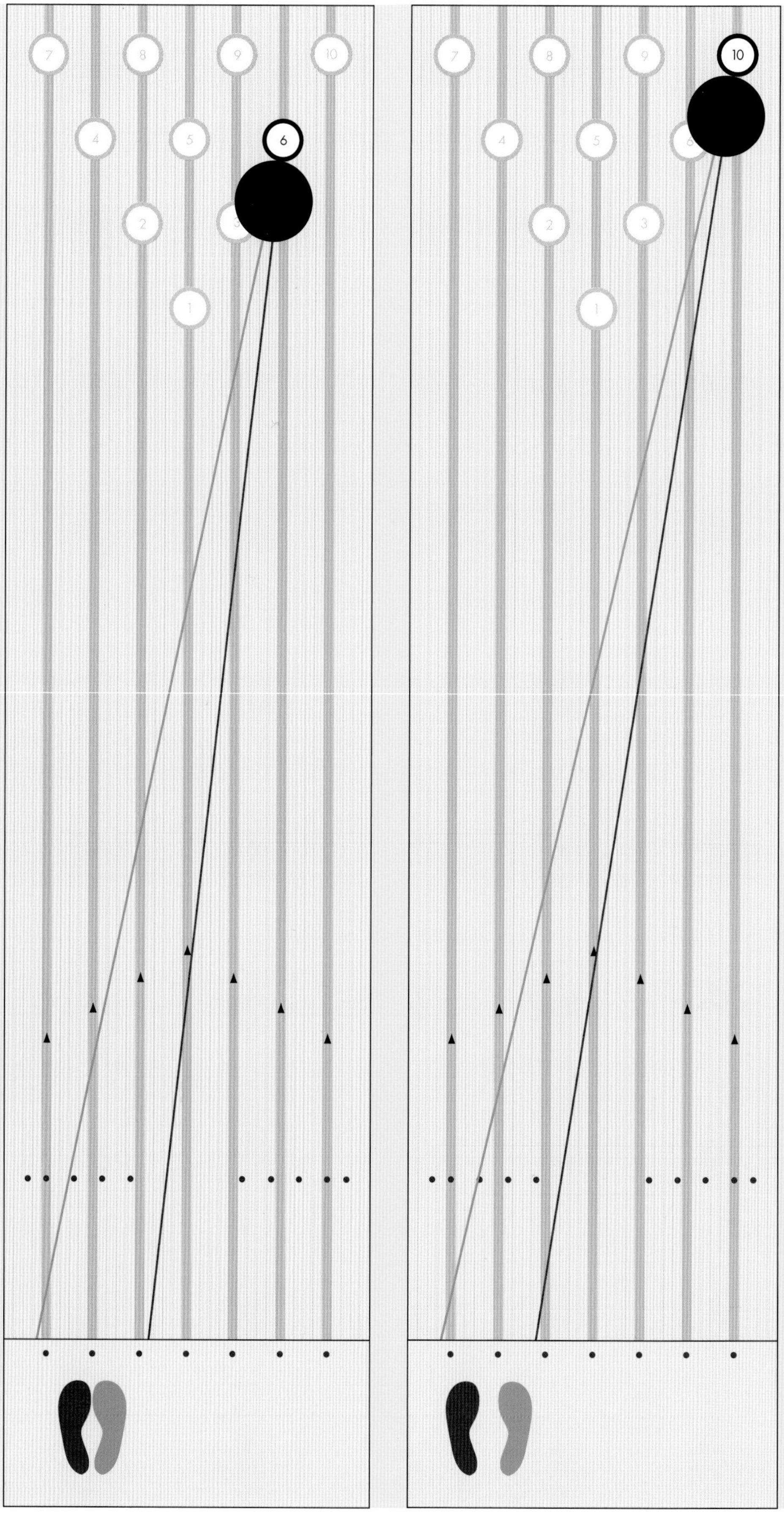

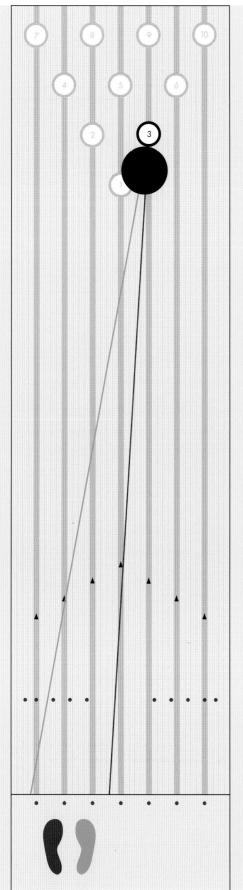

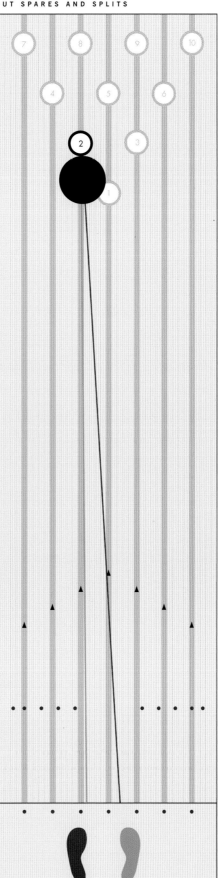

**THE STRAIGHT
SPARE SHOT**

LEFT: 3 LEAVE

RIGHT: 2 LEAVE

THE STRAIGHT SHOT

LEFT: 4-7-10 LEAVE

RIGHT: 6-7-10 LEAVE

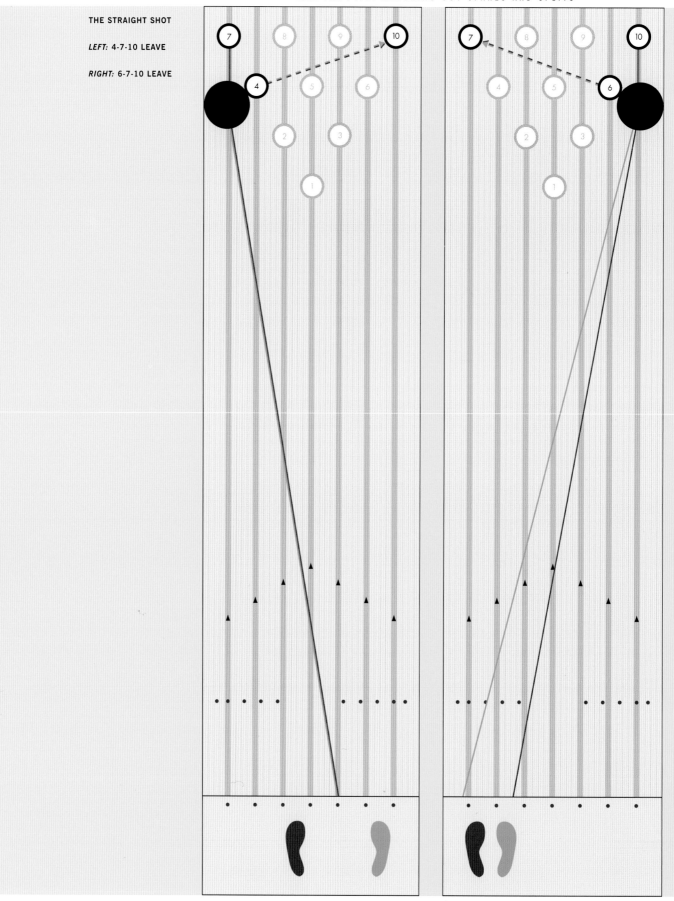

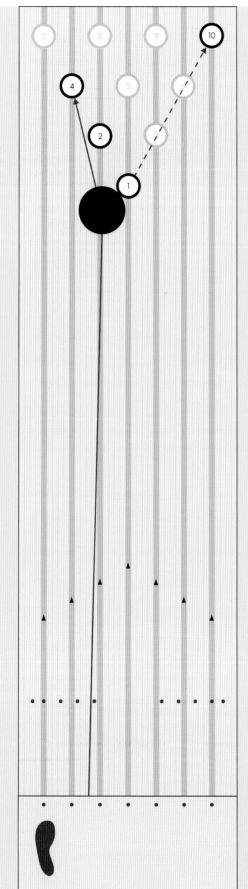

THE STRAIGHT SHOT

LEFT: THE RIGHT-
HANDER'S WASHOUT

RIGHT: THE LEFT-
HANDER'S WASHOUT

THE STRAIGHT SHOT

LEFT: THE BUCKET
FOR A RIGHT-HANDER

RIGHT: THE BUCKET
FOR A LEFT-HANDER

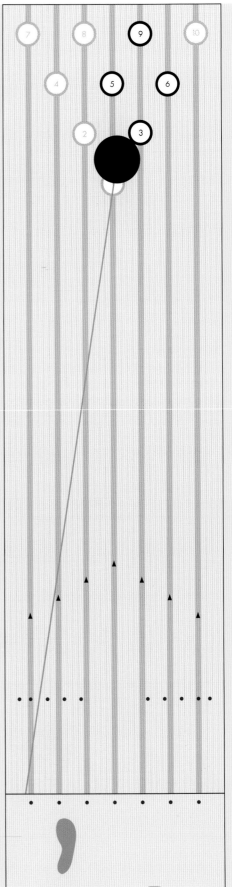

is not entirely by the book. To shoot a 7-pin I place my sliding foot on the thirtieth board during my address. I actually drift away from my center arrow target and end up sliding on the thirty-fifth board. Despite that flaw, I consider myself to be one of the better spare shooters in the sport. That's because I spend a lot of time practicing this vital aspect of the game, my armswing is consistent and straight, and I have the ability to concentrate for long periods of time so as not to take any shot for granted.

The formulas for various conversions on the following pages represent my suggestions: nothing is etched in stone. Through trial and error you will learn what works best for you. I do suggest experimenting with using one arrow for all of your left-sided spares and one arrow for all of your right-sided spares while adjusting the position of your sliding foot to accommodate each specific shot. Whether that arrow is the second, third, or fourth arrow is a matter of personal preference. Or, perhaps you wish to use different parts of the lane for different spares. What really counts is that you are comfortable after finding the formula that best suits your needs.

I do feel that it's important that the ball-return apparatus not hinder your movements. This can be a factor for a right-handed player on an even-numbered lane who is shooting at a right-sided pin (such as the 6-pin or 10-pin) or for a lefty on an odd-numbered lane who is aiming at a left-sided pin (such as the 4-pin or 7-pin). Find a target that works for all of your crosslane attempts, including those in the far corner of the lane.

Learning to go hard and straight takes time and dedication. If you're a power player, rolling in such a manner will not feel natural at first. In fact, you will probably need a few months of hard and purposeful practice to become acclimated. Don't be surprised if, during that time, your average takes a temporary dip. The investment in time and patience is worth it. Learning to master the hard-and-straight formula will take all of the guesswork out of the game no matter what the oil pattern might be. All you'll need to concentrate upon are where to stand and where to aim (see the following pages for my recommendations).

SHOOTING OFF YOUR STRIKE LINE

An alternative strategy is to shoot spares off your strike line. To do so, use your strike ball coupled with the same aiming point, release, wrist position, and speed as on your strike shot. All you change is your foot position. You can use the basic 3-6-9 Formula to calculate how much to move. First locate your target pin among those still standing. Count how many arrows away from the center arrow that this pin stands on. Multiply this number by three and you have the number of boards you should move your feet in the opposite direction of your target pin. For example, when aiming for the 2-pin, move three boards to the right (three boards to the left for a 3-pin); for the 4-pin, move six boards to the right (six boards to the left for a 6-pin); and for the 7-pin, move nine boards to the right (nine boards to the left for a 10-pin). An exception to the above rule is when shooting the 3-6-9-10 for a right-handed player or the 2-4-7-8 for a left-hander. To avoid the chop while still covering that back pin I suggest a four-board move in the opposite direction from your bowling hand.

You can use the strike line strategy when you are consistently hitting the pocket and you have observed that the oil is distributed as a favorable crown/wall on all parts of the lane. To determine how the oil is distributed on a specific lane pair, you must keenly observe your own ball's trajectory as well as the trajectories of other bowlers' balls on that lane pair. Favorable conditions for shooting spares off your strike line are often indicated by a high-scoring environment in which most players have a decent margin for error on their first shots while still being able to get their ball into the pocket.

I would caution you against employ-

EXPECT A SLIGHT DIP IN YOUR SCORING WHEN YOU START TRYING TO MASTER THE HARD-AND-STRAIGHT SHOT.

- TO USE YOUR STRIKE LINE FOR SPARES, JUST MOVE YOUR FEET BASED ON THE 3-6-9 FORMULA

- STRIKE LINE SPARE SHOTS WORK BEST WITH CROWN/WALLED OIL CONDITIONS

- USE THIS SHOT ONLY IF YOU CONSISTENTLY HIT THE POCKET WITH YOUR STRIKE SHOTS

- REALIZE THE PSCYHO-LOGICAL CHALLENGE OF REPEATING A STRIKE SHOT THAT WENT POORLY

- SINGLE-PIN SPARES ARE BEST CONVERTED WITH THE STRAIGHT SHOT

SHOOTING SPARES OFF YOUR STRIKE LINE

LEFT: 5-7 LEAVE

RIGHT: 5-10 LEAVE

THE STRIKE LINE IS SHOWN WITH A DOTTED LINE.

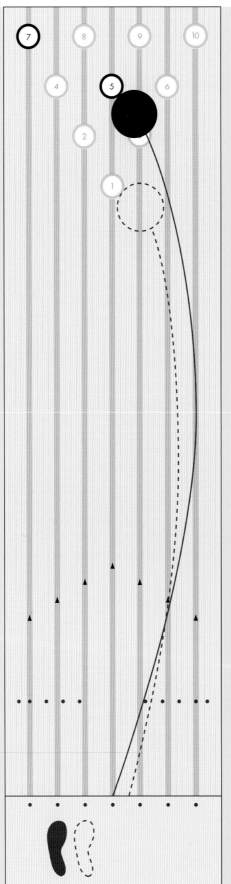

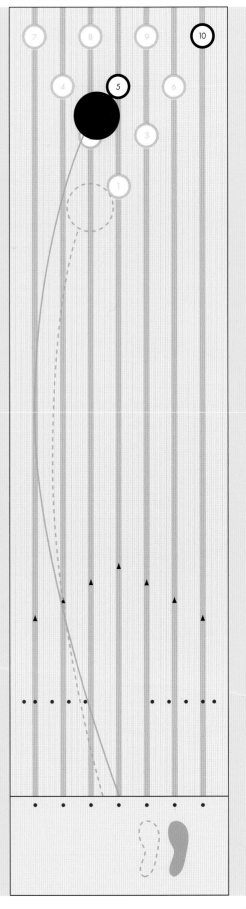

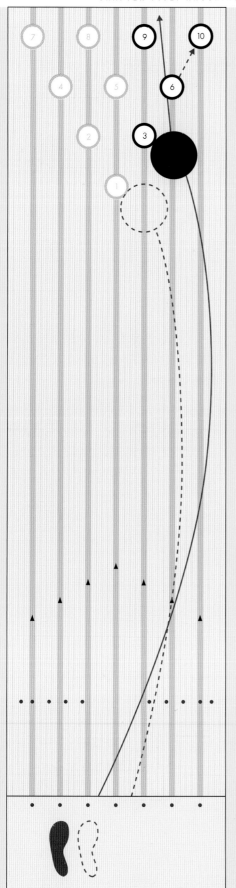

SHOOTING SPARES OFF
YOUR STRIKE LINE

LEFT: 3-6-9-10 LEAVE

RIGHT: 2-4-7-8 LEAVE

THE STRIKE LINE
IS SHOWN WITH A
DOTTED LINE.

One of the greatest challenges to bowlers at all levels of ability is to achieve consistency. I believe that the secret lies in simplicity. A delivery with minimal superfluous movements is far easier to repeat.

The principle of keeping things simple and straight was stressed by my first coach—Frank Coburn, who also taught my older sister, Kathy, and his wife, Doris, how to bowl. Dad constantly stressed fundamentals. His approach must have merit as we are the only family with three women who have each won professional titles.

He taught us that there are three vital aspects to becoming fundamentally solid. Everything starts with your pushaway. Holding the ball in line with your bowling shoulder during your address should precede handing the ball straight forward toward your target. At that juncture, your arm's muscles are disengaged. Allow gravity to force your ball to drop. Ideally, the ball will swing your arm; usually this is described as a "pendulum" armswing. Think of your arm as a string with a ball tied to its end. Although it's impossible to produce a swing totally devoid of muscular involvement, that is the ideal. The less interference, the better.

As your delivery progresses, all of your movements are parallel and your body remains perpendicular to your target. That sets up a release that pretty much occurs on its own. Your ball is released, not grabbed and pulled.

When I was five years old my mom began bowling on the tour. My parents occasionally allowed me to roll a shot, but they prohibited me from joining a youth league until they felt I'd mastered the basic form. I can still recall spending hours in our living room "bowling" without a ball. I honed the pushaway and timing using my arm's positions and synchronizing them with my footwork.

When I finally bowled for real I had a great head start.

Having a conventional style has served me well. The further any player progresses in our sport, the more important the ability to repeat becomes. I've learned that it is easier to add different types of shots and power to a repertoire if you have a solid, basic foundation upon which to build. Anyone lacking basic rhythm will find it very hard to reach the next level.

Another advantage to my simple approach is that it increases longevity. Like golf, bowling is a life-long sport. To crank shots as a twenty-five-year-old places undue stress on joints and can lead to injuries. Moreover, that style isn't very practical come middle age. In most cases, the players with the longest careers are those who cover fewer boards.

If you are a typical bowler, you don't get to the lanes as often as you would like. The more infrequently you bowl, the more important it becomes to have a simple style. True, covering a lot of boards before seeing one's ball explode into the pocket is a lot of fun. To me, though, it's even more enjoyable to knock over more pins than a player whose ultrapower style produces a feast-or-famine syndrome.

Another plus is the relative ease with which the technically correct player can pull out of a slump. We all have times when some aspect of our delivery is out of sync. The more conventional your game, the easier it is to identify and correct a problem. To be sure, there are some pros—particularly in the PBA—who aren't by the book. However, most of the players who prevail over a prolonged time actually simplify their games after coming on tour. They know that being simple is simply smart.

ing this tactic if there is a segment of the lane that is severely dry or wet. For example: You are playing up the second arrow. You have noticed that your ball hooks early and radically when drifting wide of the eighth board (severely dry) but it hardly moves when inside of the twelfth board (extreme oil). Thus, a three-board move in either direction would greatly alter the shot's subsequent trajectory.

I also wouldn't go this route unless I have demonstrated the ability to repeat shots and consistently hit my target. This strategy isn't for you if your strike ball isn't hitting the pocket on average at least eight times a game.

Another problem with strike line spare shooting is psychological. Let's say you have just left the bucket—the 2-4-5-8 for a right-handed bowler or the 3-5-6-9 for a left-handed player. Obviously, your first shot in that frame wasn't very good. You now must fully put that poor delivery out of your mind and not compensate with a physical change from your normal strike ball when trying to cover the spare. For what it's worth, I almost always use the hard-and-straight strategy when shooting the bucket. To cover the back pin, I simply use a crosslane angle. Most right-handers prefer to go fairly straight between the fourth and the fifth arrows.

Experiment with using both strategies (hard-and-straight and strike line). Through trial and error you will discover which works best for you. I can tell you that I can't think of any top pro star who hooks the ball at his or her spares, with the exception of a few players who do so at some double-wood combinations. While you can shoot your spares using your strike line, it doesn't mean that you should do so. There is a case to be made for using your strike line when double wood is involved and, thus, some power is necessary to avoid your ball deflecting to miss the back pin when it arrives at the target pin off center.

For single-pin spares, however, you are sacrificing what you do need (accura-cy) for what isn't required (power). The greater the number of boards that your ball covers, the more accuracy is needlessly being sacrificed. While, in theory, almost any spare can be converted using the 3-6-9 formula, the near-sided corner pin (the 10-pin for a right-handed player and the 7-pin for a lefty) and the 6-10 (righty) and the 4-7 (lefty) are very problematic.

Regardless of which tactic works better for you, it is vital that you consistently fill frames. I can state without fear of contradiction that my strike ball is not the best on the tour. In fact, it's not even close. Much of my edge comes from filling frames as well as anyone. During the three decades that I've been a pro I have seen dozens of wannabes come and go who could out-strike me. That's because a player who opens after a double is under par while a rival who alternates strikes and spares with but one double will roll in the 200s.

Ironically, the first time I had to make a shot to capture a PBA title, what stood between me and the trophy was a 7-pin. Had that occurred a few years before, against Charlie, there was a good chance that I'd have whiffed. But all of that practice paid dividends. I made it with ease to beat Scott Devers.

No matter at what level you compete—from being a once-a-month mixed-league participant to a highly ambitious and competitive bowler—you will find that players who don't beat themselves enjoy a great advantage. I can't sufficiently stress just how important Charlie's and Mark's advice has been to my success. What they told me is every bit as applicable to you. If you consistently cover your spares you will find your average rising significantly. After all, it's possible to post a 190 score without rolling a single strike. And that's not too shabby!

TO ALTER THE AMOUNT OF YOUR SHOTS' HOOK, CHANGE YOUR WRIST POSITION: CUPPED PRODUCES THE MOST HOOK WHILE BENT BACKWARD PRODUCES THE LEAST HOOK.

CHAPTER SIX: DEVELOPING STRATEGIES

E very high-level player and most league bowlers have an individual strategy for one or two favorite balls and a specific line to the pocket. Whenever feasible, we all will opt to bowl our A-game. However, there are occasions when you will discover that the lane conditions are highly unfavorable to your strategy of choice.

It is often said that a good golfer has many clubs in his bag. So, too, a good bowler should have many strategies at his disposal. You should be able to recognize evolving oil patterns and to craft the appropriate strategy that will provide your subsequent deliveries with the greatest margin for error. While being able to do so becomes increasingly important as you climb up bowling's competitive ladder, if you are a league player who is carrying an average in the 150-to-190 range you should work to develop a B-game. In fact, if you are sufficiently skilled to be able to hook the ball, you are capable of playing different parts of the lane without taking a hit on the scoresheet.

READING THE LANE

Having scouted how successful members of the previous squad were playing the lanes, I can enter my warm-up armed with an educated guess as to which strategies are the most likely to work and which ones I should probably discard. Like you, whenever possible I prefer to utilize my A-game.

Your job is never done simply when the ball has left your hand. As soon as that ball hits the lane you are transformed from a bowler to your own bowling critic and coach. You must watch your shot intently. Did it roll over your target? Where did it make contact against the pins? Did your strike shot possess ample energy when it reached its destination or did it deflect off the pins like a wet dishrag? Taking note of the above factors is vital if you are to correct any flaw. Every shot ought to teach you something that is applicable to subsequent deliveries.

My favorite strike line shot would see me sliding anywhere from the thirteenth to the fifteenth board. I aim for the first arrow. My ball will continue toward the channel and reach the second or third board as it stops skidding and starts to roll. About two-thirds (forty feet) to three-quarters (forty-five feet) of the way down the lane my shot will start hooking back powerfully as it gathers momentum and begins its trajectory toward the pocket. I have a fairly late break point and a pronounced hook.

In contrast, given his druthers Jason Couch will play deep inside and hook most of the lane. What makes both Jason and me successful is that we can be competitive when forced to utilize our so-called B-game. I have won while playing the third arrow, and Jason has lifted trophies after playing up the boards. Being versatile is what separates players who enjoy long and productive careers, such as Mike Aulby, from pros who have one or two big years and then fade from the scene as conditions evolve.

Versatility is even more important for those of you who are right-handed than it is for us southpaws. That's because there are so many more righties that your side of the lane tends to break down quicker and more often.

There are occasions when it is absolutely apparent that the lanes are moderately wet or dry and all that's required is a change of ball to stay within my primary comfort zone. On the other hand, I often face situations in which the conditions might seem more forgiving in a different area of the lane. In these cases there is just no way for me to be able to play as I would normally choose while remaining competitive with the tournament's leaders.

As helpful as it is to observe and talk with players from the previous squad, to truly ascertain what the lane conditions are like, you must bowl a few practice shots. Throw your first shot at about sixty percent of your normal effort, just to prepare your body for the task at hand. This is important for all players but especially so for us middle-aged and senior players. To impart full force before your muscles are loose is to risk an injury. A prebowling stretching regimen, while highly recommended, is not sufficient in and of itself to ready yourself to roll all-out. Slowly increase the force imparted until you determine that it's safe to utilize all of your force. The number of shots required to reach that point will depend on many factors, including how you're feeling and even the weather conditions.

By my third shot I am ready to get to work. I use my "benchmark" ball. It's a midrange option that hooks moderately. I then concentrate just as fully as I will during the upcoming competition because I know that I can obtain an accurate read on the conditions only if I execute my movements the same way that I intend to do once the game begins. As a professional, I have several balls at my disposal. Each has subtle differences that distinguish it from the others. They run the entire rainbow, with incremental changes from some that hook a lot to others that hardly grab the lane at all (see

- IN YOUR WARM-UP, IDENTIFY THE BEST BALL, STRIKE LINE, AND RELEASE FOR THE LANE

- EXPERIMENT WITH BALL CHOICE

- TRY OUT A BACKUP STRIKE LINE

- ATTEMPT TO DISCOVER HOW MUCH AREA YOU HAVE TO WORK WITH

- USE YOUR SPARE STRAIGHT SHOT FOR THE 7- AND 10-PINS

- MOVE YOUR FEET AND TARGET INWARD TO TRY OUT OTHER STRIKE LINES

- THE TRACK SHOT, THE MOST COMMON OIL CONDITION, EXISTS WHEN A POPULAR STRIKE LINE HAS WORN A TRACK INTO THE OIL THAT GUIDES YOUR SHOT TO THE POCKET

- WALLED OIL CONDITIONS MEAN THE OUTSIDE BOARDS ARE VERY DRY WHILE THE CENTER IS HEAVILY OILED, WHICH GUIDES THE BALL TO THE POCKET

- OVERBLOCKED CONDITIONS HAVE A DRASTIC AMOUNT OF OIL CLOSE TO DRY BOARDS AND CREATE A WIDE DRIFT

- REVERSE BLOCK CONDITIONS MEANS OIL IS CONCENTRATED ON THE OUTSIDE BOARDS WITH THE CENTER DRY, WHICH MAKES MOST SHOTS HARD

LEFT:
THE BOHN A-GAME
STRIKE LINE

THE SHOT I PREFER
INVOLVES SLIDING MY
FOOT AROUND THE
FOURTEENTH BOARD
AND AIMING FOR THE
FIRST ARROW. THE
BALL WILL SKID
TOWARD THE GUTTER,
THEN ROLL STRAIGHT
DOWN, AND THEN
HOOK POWERFULLY
INWARD ABOUT
THREE-QUARTERS OF
THE WAY DOWN
THE LANE.

RIGHT:
INSIDE STRIKE LINES

THIS SHOT CAN BE
PLAYED FROM ANY
POINT AS FAR INSIDE
AS YOU WOULD LIKE.
THIS SHOWS JUST ONE
EXAMPLE. THE ULTRA-
POWER PLAYER
WHOSE SHOT HAS
LESS ACUCURACY BUT
PRODUCES MAXIMUM
HOOK AND BALL REVS,
GENERALLY FOLLOWS
A DEEP INSIDE
STRIKE LINE.

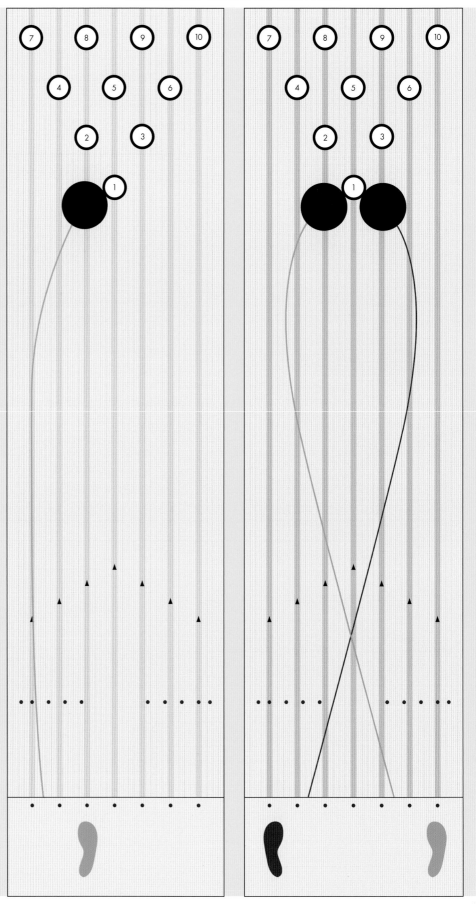

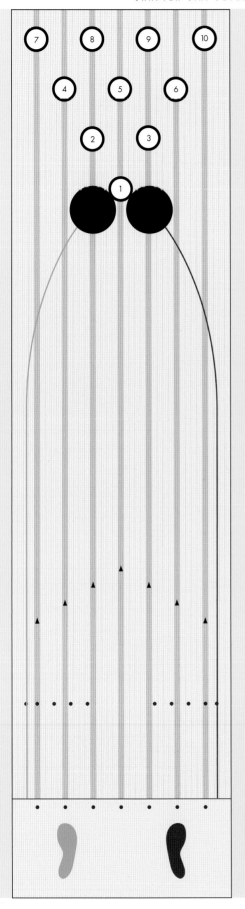

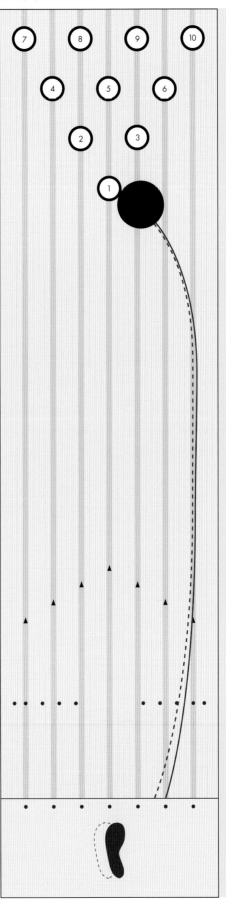

LEFT:
OUTSIDE STRIKE LINES

THIS SHOT IS ALSO
REFERRED TO AS THE
GUTTER SHOT OR
"PLAYING UP THE
BOARDS." WITH THIS
SHOT, YOUR TARGET
BOARD IS THE SAME
AS THE BOARD ON
WHICH YOU RELEASE
THE BALL. THE HIGH-
ACCURACY SMOOTH
STROKER PLAYER
TENDS TO
USE AN OUTSIDE
STRIKE LINE.

RIGHT:
THE TWO-AND-ONE
ADJUSTMENT
(RIGHT-HANDED)

WHEN YOUR BALL
DRIFTS HIGH AFTER
WHAT YOU FELT WAS A
GOOD SHOT, MAKE
THIS ADJUSTMENT. AS
OIL TENDS TO DISSI-
PATE AFTER PLAY ON
THE LANES, YOUR
SHOT WILL BEGIN
HOOKING MORE. TO
ADJUST FOR THESE
DRY CONDITIONS,
MOVE YOUR FEET TWO
BOARDS AND YOUR
TARGET ONE BOARD
TO THE INSIDE. THE
DOTTED LINE SHOWS
THE ADJUSTMENT.

LEFT:
THE TRACK IN
THE LANE

MOST LANES DEVELOP
TRACKS WHERE
THE MAJORITY OF
BOWLERS ROLL THEIR
BALLS AND WHERE
THE OIL HAS BEEN
WORN DOWN.
IT'S BEST TO AVOID
THE TRACK.

RIGHT:
THE WALLED LANE

WHEN THE OUTSIDE
BOARDS ARE DRY AND
THE CENTER IS OILY,
YOUR SHOT IS GUIDED
INTO THE POCKET.

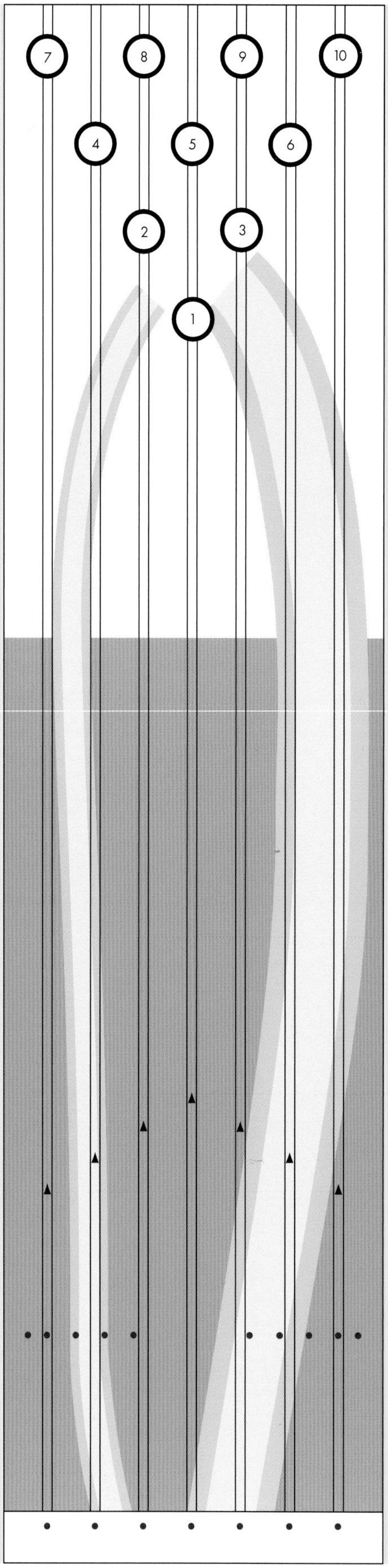

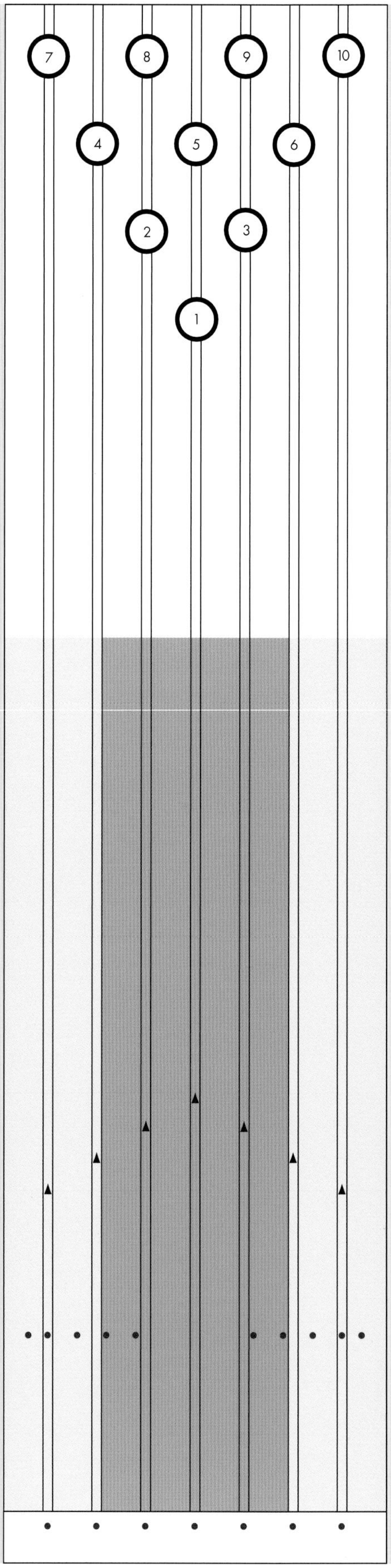

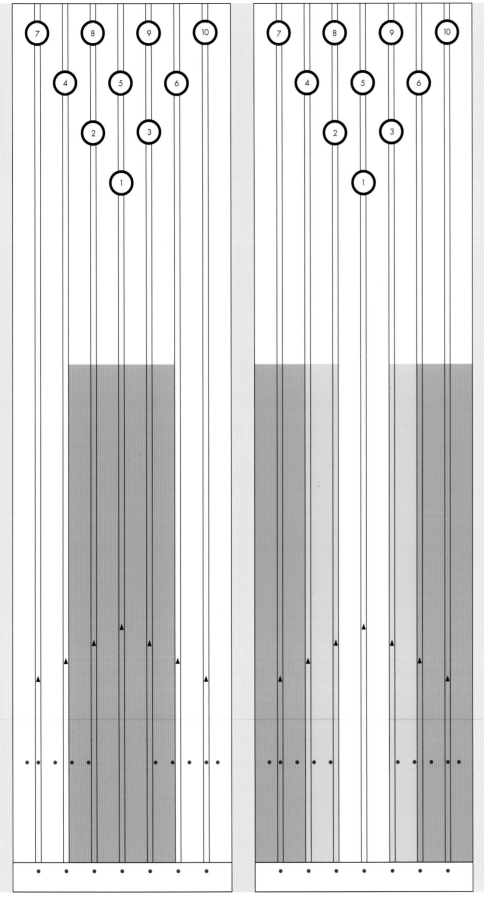

LEFT:
THE OVERBLOCKED LANE

THIS MEANS THERE IS A LOT OF OIL VERY CLOSE TO DRY BOARDS, A CONDITION FAVORABLE FOR PLAYERS WITH A STRONG STRAIGHT SHOT.

RIGHT:
THE REVERSE BLOCK

WHEN HEAVY OIL IS CONCENTRATED ON THE OUTSIDE BOARDS AND THE CENTER IS DRIER, HITTING THE POCKET IS DIFFICULT FOR MOST PLAYERS. THIS CONDITION IS FAVORABLE FOR A BOWLER WHO PLAYS DEEP INSIDE WITH A GOOD AMOUNT OF HOOK.

chapter two for a detailed discussion of ball composition). By using my benchmark ball I should immediately be able to tell if I need to switch to a ball that hooks more or less and, if so, whether I am in need of a drastic, moderate, or infinitesimal change. At this stage I also determine which balls are unlikely to be required for the upcoming block. Those ones will quickly be dispatched to the paddock as I have no great desire to unnecessarily lug several sixteen-pound balls following every game.

If I really like how my strike line is performing on a given lane and am confident that it will remain productive throughout the upcoming block, I may experiment with my equipment. Using an educated guess, I try a ball that I feel has the potential to provide a greater margin for error or to carry half-hits more efficiently.

In the best of all worlds, you will quickly find a ball, release, and strike line combination with which you are confident and comfortable. You now have several options of how to continue your warm-up. The first, which I recommend, is to experiment with a backup strike line. But do this only if you have been consistently filling frames and you anticipate that the oil on the lanes might change during your round. The more games you must bowl, the more likely it is that the oil will migrate. This is especially likely if you're right-handed, since your side of the lane will almost assuredly be seeing a lot more action than does my neighborhood. Having tested out your backup strike line you will be prepared for the oil change.

Another option is to see how much area is at your disposal when using your normal strike line. "Area" refers to the lateral distance at which you can miss your target (either to the left or the right) and still hit the pocket. There is nothing that loosens up the ol' armswing quite like knowing that you have several boards with which to work. This, too, can only be ascertained through trial and error. In my case, I'll stand in my normal

place (so as to slide between thirteen and fifteen) and aim halfway between the gutter and the first arrow (the third board) on one shot and midway between the first and second arrows (the seventh board) on the next. Ideally, the former will see the 4-pin nudge over the 7-pin, and the latter will trip the 6-pin. If that occurs, look out, world, 'cause here I come!

A third option to try is to practice a corner spin spare shot on either side. Using at least a shot apiece to practice covering the 10-pin and the 7-pin has an added benefit. Watch your ball intently as it rolls down the lane. Even though you are attempting to produce a straight-as-an-arrow shot, your ball will provide some relevant information. Notice if it gets into a roll earlier or later than anticipated. Also, if a giant oil ring exists on the ball following the shot you know that there is a lot of oil somewhere on the lane. That might dictate what moves to avoid, and could make you cautious about attempting to convert a spare off your strike line.

If you have found that your A-game line works, one more thing you can try in your practice shots is to move both your feet and your target inward (to the right for us lefties and vice-versa for right-handers). A note to my fellow southpaws: only rarely would my release point be farther inside than the fourth arrow, as we almost always wish to avoid the parts of the lane that are getting the most play, whereas right-handers may move in as deep as the sixth or seventh arrows for their strike line.

By the conclusion of practice you should have established a clear-cut spot from which to play and determine which ball in your arsenal will yield the highest scores. The key is to have learned enough during the warm-up phase that you enter the competitive portion of the block brimming with confidence. Every bowler has a mental image of what his or her shot looks like when it has been rolled just right. To make an adjustment it is essential that you read how your ball

ABOVE: GEORGE BRANHAM III, THE 1993 FIRESTONE TOURNAMENT OF CHAMPIONS WINNER, WATCHES CLOSELY AS HIS BALL ROLLS DOWN THE LANE. ALWAYS OBSERVE HOW YOUR BALL REACTS TO THE LANE IN ORDER TO KNOW HOW BEST TO MAKE YOUR NEXT SHOT.

is reacting to the lane. The most obvious observation is assessing how much or how little your shots are hooking, but there is much more data to factor into the equation. I also try to ascertain if my ball is grabbing the lane prematurely, in mid-lane, belatedly, or if it fails to hook alto-gether. I analyze the results of any shots that stray either inside or outside of my target to learn just how they're reacting. The greater the margin for error, the more advantageous it is to play that line.

There are several common oil pat-terns you will be able to identify with your warm-up practice shots. Of these, most bowlers prefer the conditions that allow them to use the track shot. I esti-mate that about half of the houses in which I've competed feature a definitive track shot. In most of those centers, the track is found between the second and third arrows for right-handed bowlers and between the first and second arrows for lefties. The track shot is simply the part of the lane where most bowlers' balls have gone down the lane, wearing a groove of sorts into the oil. Here the ball will roll down the lane proportionately, making a steady move toward the pock-et. Ideally, the track will provide "hold." This means that any shot that is slightly inside your target avoids hitting the nose or going Brooklyn (that is, to the left of the headpin for a right-hander and and to the right of the headpin for a left-han-der). Equally important is that the track shot provides ample "swing." This means that a shot that misses wide of your target is still able to get back to the pocket.

Maximum scoring potential exists when the lanes are "walled." With the outside boards very dry and the very cen-ter of the lane heavily oiled, it's almost as if you have to try to miss the pocket to avoid striking. Any target that you miss wide will nevertheless see your shot roar-ing back into play. Conversely, if you are inaccurate toward the center of the lane, the considerable concentration of oil will counter your shot's natural inclination to drift high. On a walled condition most every good player will hit the pocket con-

sistently. Thus, under walled conditions, winning is generally determined not by a bowler's accuracy but rather by a bowler's ability to carry all the pins once the ball comes into the pocket. Use the ball that hits the best and that provides you with the greatest amount

of confidence.

An overblocked condition, which is especially challenging for hook players, creates what is known as an over/under pattern. This means there is a drastic amount of oil on and immediately inside of and adjacent to the drier boards (which are nearer the channels). If the ball drifts wide it overreacts and will hit the nose or go Brooklyn. A shot missing inside (where there is ample oil)

ABOVE: THE APPROXI-MATE FOOT POSITION OF A LEFT-HANDER'S SLIDING FOOT FOR AN INSIDE STRIKE SHOT.

THE "TEXTBOOK"
FORM THAT HAS
HELPED PARKER
SUCCEED.

could fail to hook altogether. Thus, power players opting for an inside line will likely experience havoc on any inaccurate delivery.

Also known as ten-to-ten, this can be a fantastic condition for down-and-in players who possess a clean release. Conversely, a power player who is using the wrong ball will find it nearly impossible to hit the pocket twice in a row. Other varieties include two-to-two, fifteen-to-fifteen, and anything in between. Ten-to-ten means that the only areas of the lane that aren't flooded are the ten boards nearest the gutter on either side of the lane. While this represents the cranker's toughest challenge, it is nirvana for straight players. Their advantage derives from their ability to keep their shots in play and, thus, to avert many open frames.

A reverse block condition assures that scoring will be lower than normal. Heavy oil can be found to the outside on each side of the lane, usually getting drier toward the second or the third arrow. Meanwhile, the middle boards are either relatively or extremely dry.

WHAT'S MY LINE?

Reverse Block Lanes
On a reverse block the majority of pros counter the condition by playing deep inside, using the fourth arrow (or even deeper) as their target. This line is recommended when there is excessive oil on the outside, when your shot that was aimed outside hooks too soon, or when you can find a little bit of hold and some swing that allows you to get to the pocket consistently. This is the line mainly utilized by right-handed crankers when the lanes break down. They find it helpful to use the smoothest part of the head. Additionally, by moving inside they are able to find more front-end oil to help get their shot down the lane to prevent a premature roll.

You will be able to recognize this situation when you see your ball making the transition from skid to roll too soon. Early hook calls for increasing loft and

ball speed, adjusting your hand to a less cupped position, or, the simplest solution of all, moving farther inside. The latter is my choice, because making a change in how you deliver your shots risks sacrificing rhythm, timing, and the consistency of your release.

While a right-handed bowler moves to the left, it doesn't always mean that we lefties should keep moving to our right. If the right side has broken down, we could be moving into bowling quicksand. When the inside line doesn't prove to be the solution, a left-handed player might be forced to go far outside and play the gutter. Should you give that a try, only to find that your ball never hooks, return inside and attempt to make the best of it.

The Gutter Shot
Generally speaking, the most efficient angle from which to carry is when your shot roars into the pocket from the gutter. This is the angle in which a light shot most often produces the messenger hit (when the headpin rebounds off the far side wall and sweeps across the lane to eliminate the near-sided corner pin) and the wall shot (when the headpin ricochets off the far side wall before eliminating the 4-5-7 for a righty or the 5-6-10 for a left-hander).

When a strong release creates a good roll you will find that you slap out a lot of corner pins (the 10-pin for righties and the 7-pin for lefties). Whenever you see the 7-pin toppling inward, you know that the ball came off your hand cleanly. If the ball hung even a little bit and you missed inside to cause your shot to drift high only to trip the 6-pin (4-pin for right-handers), you will feel like you can conquer the world.

One of the greatest advantages of playing the gutter is that it allows you to swing the ball slightly as the lanes begin to break down. That's because there is usually ample oil to be found. When playing up the boards your shoulders and hips should be square (parallel) to the foul line. You release the ball from and aim it for the same-numbered board.

- WITH REVERSE BLOCK LANES, PLAY DEEP INSIDE

- USE A GUTTER SHOT FOR THE MOST EFFICIENT PIN CARRY

- RELEASE AND AIM ON THE SAME BOARD WHEN THERE IS A LOT OF OIL

- RELEASE ON A HIGH-NUMBER BOARD AND AIM FOR A LOW-NUMBER BOARD WHEN YOU'RE A POWER BOWLER

- IF YOU MISS RIGHT, MOVE RIGHT ON THE BOARDS; IF YOU MISS LEFT, MOVE LEFT ON THE BOARDS

- MAKE ADJUSTMENTS ONLY IF YOU'RE SURE OIL CHANGES ARE CAUSING YOUR PROBLEM

- USE THE TWO-AND-ONE MOVE WHEN THE OIL BREAKS DOWN

- MOVE YOUR EYES FARTHER DOWN THE LANE WHEN OIL BREAKS DOWN

TO DELAY YOUR BREAK POINT AND SLIGHTLY DECREASE YOUR SHOT'S OVERALL HOOK, MAINTAIN THE SAME BOARD AS A TARGET BUT AIM FARTHER DOWN THE LANE.

ABOVE: THE THIRD PLAYER TO HAVE CAPTURED THIRTY PBA TOUR TITLES, WALTER RAY WILLIAMS JR. EXPERTLY USES THE SIDE CUPPED HAND POSITION TO HIS ADVANTAGE WHEN CONDITIONS CALL FOR A BALL WITH VERY LITTLE HOOK.

Thus, if you are aiming for the second arrow (10th board), the ball is also released on the 10th board. This is a solid option when the lanes are tight, allowing you to hold a line to the pocket. Your ball goes up the lane to get it into an earlier roll so that your shot will turn over. As a result, your ball maintains ample speed as it enters the pocket. This strategy is often referred to as "not giving the pocket away." You will recognize when to go this route by noting that any shot that is swung wide has refused to come back.

Swinging the Ball
Swinging the ball—also known as opening up the lane—refers to when you slide on a higher-numbered board and aim for a lower-numbered one. In this case, your shoulders and hips open up considerably during your backswing and remain slightly open at the point of release. Project the ball across the boards to produce the desired initial inside-to-outside trajectory. Your ball moves away from the pocket until it's about three-quarters (forty-five feet) down the lane. At that point the roll ends and the hooking action commences. The advantage of this tactic is that power players can usually create more area for themselves on most conditions. While the strength of the roll is more important than pinpoint accuracy, you will gain a competitive edge only if you don't incessantly spray shots. The tradeoff between power and control can't be so extreme that you have so much of the former that you are unable to hit the broadside of a barn.

Oil Breakdown
Oil, by its nature, is transient. As it moves, the lane condition is altered. In the old days, as a block unfolded the lane usually began to hook slightly more. The lane was predictable, and the subsequent adjustment was simple. "If you miss right, move right; if you miss left, move left." That advice, first told to me when I was a preteen, constituted my introduction to lane adjustment strategies. In many situations today, the appropriate

adjustment is no more complicated than that. If your shot is two boards light of the pocket you will rectify the situation simply by using the same target while moving your feet about two boards in the direction of your bowling hand. The only catch is that you only adjust after executing a satisfactory delivery that results in hitting your target with the same roll and speed as on your other shots.

But things aren't always that simple. There are several factors that explain why some of today's changes tend to be far more drastic. The ultra-powerful bowling balls now on the market absorb and redistribute the oil far more dramatically than did their predecessors. With each shot, more oil is moved. Some of it ends up on your ball. The rest of it is redistributed farther down the lane, or it evaporates.

If you were to walk down a freshly resurfaced lane following a few games of use you would discover a series of oil strips about a quarter of an inch to two inches long and roughly a sixteenth of an inch wide. Known as carrydown, this phenomenon hinders the ability of a shot to finish. Thus, it is visually apparent that a ball that was hooking dramatically early on the backend in a block has its trajectory straightened out as it nears the pindeck. By carefully analyzing and observing each of your shots you will determine if your ball's reaction has changed due to a physical cause (your release, ball speed, or accuracy were compromised on that delivery) or because of oil migration. Make an adjustment only if you are confident that it's the latter. Another factor contributing to today's dramatic lane transition is the frequency with which lanes are now stripped. In the 1960s and '70s the typical house would fully clean each alley and then reapply oil on a weekly basis. By the middle of the week so much oil had moved that the changes during a tournament block or three games of league play would be minute and involve very basic adjustments.

Machines are now capable of carrying out the formerly laborious task of stripping the facility, so it is no longer uncommon for a center to strip all of its lanes daily. Thus, during the course of a league's play the backend might transform from completely dry to having some oily portions. Even though manufacturers have introduced thicker oil to limit the migration, the trend is still exacerbated when several players are using a similar strike line. That's why a right-handed player generally must be more versatile than those who are rolling on the far-less-used opposite side of the lane.

Lanes that aren't stripped regularly present a different challenge. Their backends will become excessively tight. While there won't be as dramatic a transition while you compete, your ability to carry half-hits will be severely challenged.

Carrydown usually inhibits scoring. However, there are times when it helps a power player by creating a "hold" area. Straighter shooters tend to struggle, especially as their shots deflect after entering the pocket to produce a lot of weak hits. The best advice is to move outside, slightly decrease your ball speed, and keep your shots in play.

The Two-and-One Move
Most moves are small and incremental. During the course of your league or tournament play it is likely that the lanes will cause your ball to hook more as the oil slowly dissipates. Suddenly, the same shot that shattered the pins a few frames ago is drifting high (that is, to the left side of the headpin for a right-hander or vice versa for a lefty). You are faced with a 4-pin (for a right-handed player) or a 6-pin (left-handed). The most common and most simple adjustment is what's known as a two-and-one move: your feet move two boards to the inside (to the left for a right-handed player and vice-versa), while you alter your target one board in the same direction. This will pick up just enough early oil to slightly delay your hook, while still allowing your shot to finish powerfully.

Power players have larger target zones than do those who tend to rely more upon accuracy. Thus, a cranker might be more inclined to use a three-and-two move or, even, a four-and-two.

As little as a half of a board can make a difference. A right-handed player moving that amount to the right can be the remedy for slapping out that pesky 10-pin. What to do if that move results in a slightly high hit with a 4-pin leave? I recommend going back to your original line coupled with moving about six inches backwards on the approach while maintaining the same ball speed. That should allow your shot to drift fractionally higher in the pocket than the one that had left the 10-pin. Stand slightly farther inside when you seek to counter shots that are drifting slightly high, so as not to be faced with a 4-pin (righty) or a 6-pin (lefty) leave.

When the lanes are very tight and your ball is refusing to "read" the lane, try moving your starting position six to twelve inches closer to the foul line. This should force you to take shorter strides, which will result in a decrease in ball speed. Hopefully, your ball will now hook an additional three to seven boards.

Another option is to move your eyes. This strategy involves maintaining the same target board, but to aim farther down the lane at a point that is beyond the arrows. Doing so will delay the break point and, with it, the amount of arc on your shot. Conversely, when your shots are slightly light you can move your target closer to the foul line, which will cause earlier ball roll to produce a bit more hook. Please note that with any (and all) of these moves, you must attempt to maintain the same ball speed.

WRIST ALTERATIONS

How much or little your wrist is cocked, coupled with your hand position, also changes ball reaction. The common—or flat—position provides for a normal roll. Neophyte and lower-average players will naturally keep to this position in which the wrist continues in a straight line with the lower arm. Any player with a con-

TO HASTEN YOUR BREAK POINT AND SLIGHTLY INCREASE YOUR SHOT'S OVERALL HOOK, MAINTAIN THE SAME BOARD AS A TARGET BUT AIM CLOSER TO THE FOUL LINE.

ABOVE: TWO-TIME PBA PLAYER OF THE YEAR AND HALL OF FAME MEMBER AMLETO MONACELLI IS A MASTER AT EXPLOITING BALL ROLLOUT WHEN THE LANE CONDITIONS MERIT USING IT.

ventional grip will do so as well.

To cup your wrist is to bring your fingers in toward your palm. This position is maintained throughout the entire armswing. The intention is to quicken your thumb's exit, to allow your fingers to impart greater "hit" during the release, resulting in a stronger roll and larger hook. This is recommended on tighter lanes and when you want your ball to react to the midpoint (sixteen to thirty feet from the foul line) of the lane.

has rolled out (lacking sufficient carrying power). The telltale sign of rollout is when you see that your ball mysteriously stops hooking as it approaches the pocket. In general, this is not a desired reaction although Amleto Monacelli has made a Hall of Fame career out of intentionally having his shots roll out and it certainly hasn't harmed Steve Hoskins, either. The side cupped position is best on extreme conditions (severe or no hook). The outside grip features a flat

It will allow your ball to "read" the center of the lane. It's also needed when you're hitting the pocket, but leave a succession of soft/weak 10-pins (right-handers) or soft/weak 7-pins (lefties).

The side cupped position involves a cupped wrist, with your hand on the outside of the ball. It is ideal for when you want your ball to skid farther through the head portion of the lane to avoid getting into a premature roll/hook. This is important when you notice that your ball

ABOVE: JASON COUCH, THE 1999 WINNER OF THE BRUNSWICK WORLD TOURNAMENT OF CHAMPIONS, HAS BECOME FAR MORE VERSATILE WITH EXPERIENCE.

wrist. Place your hand on the outside of your ball with your palm facing inward while your wrist is straight. This is used when the lanes are either excessively wet or dry outside your target or when your ball fails to come back after encountering heavy oil far down the lane. This release maximizes control and produces just a moderate break at the backend. For you tour fans, watch Walter Ray Williams Jr. when this release is appropriate, as he is absolutely its master.

The least-used option for strike shots is the broken wrist grip. It is designed to minimize hook. Most often seen on very dry lanes, it is also appropriate for spare conversion attempts.

JUDGMENT PARAMETERS

Every football coach knows that there is a time to gamble and a time to punt. So should you. Being stubborn as a mule can be a very costly character flaw in our sport. When the lane conditions are extreme, you have to recognize that you might not be able to hit your average. However, that's no problem if you are sufficiently smart and versatile that you can still shoot only ten pins below your norm while others are losing thirty sticks. Let's say that the lanes are extremely oily. The natural tendency is to attempt to put as much "juice" as you can on your strike shots. Avoid that temptation. In this case, less is more. Keep your armswing loose and be smooth. Rotate your hand around the ball gently during your release, with your eyes riveted on your target. Execute a smooth exit and follow-through. Do not try to hit on the ball lest excessive skid will result.

Being a top-level bowler is like being a successful stockbroker—you have lots of options! But when do you decide to change equipment, alter your hand and wrist position, change your strike line, or modify your ball speed or loft? The answers are most often gleaned through experience and observation.

My recommendation is that, when in doubt, try moving your feet first. This is the most simple alteration and it allows you to maintain your delivery's natural rhythm, timing, and tempo. If this doesn't prove fruitful, higher-average players can then switch their equipment and/or hand/wrist positions. Elite players also move their feet first followed by switching equipment and/or hand/wrist positions. Their final option is to adjust ball speed and/or loft. I am not suggesting that only the elite bowler experiment with ball speed/loft changes. You can try it but only if you have worked on it extensively in practice and are able to make such a change without throwing your delivery off-kilter.

As a general rule, I switch balls when I feel like I'm fighting what's out there. I want to enjoy my time on the lanes. I am sufficiently open-minded to realize that the ball that worked in the morning might not be useful that night. Having tried the more subtle moves on the lane while using the same equipment, clearly it is now time to swap balls.

In general, scoring conditions dictate your actions. The lower the scoring environment, the more direct your route to the pocket should be. The more pins are falling, the more boards you can attempt to cover.

The top-level players make moves almost instinctively. Our versatility and experience provide us with a great advantage. That's why the true test of greatness on either the PBA or the PWBA tours is the test of time. A good player might have a great tournament or even a great run of events. But the truly great player does it year after year despite changes in equipment and lane conditions. The final word on strategy is to employ the KISS system. When in doubt, Keep It Simple, (or you're being) Stupid. The more radical the change, the less likely you will be to guess correctly and the less likely you will be to repeat your shots.

- USE A FLAT WRIST FOR A NORMAL ROLL
- USE A CUPPED WRIST FOR LARGER HOOK ON OILY LANES
- USE A SIDE CUPPED POSITION TO AVOID A PREMATURE ROLL AND HOOK
- USE A BROKEN WRIST GRIP FOR DRY LANES

- WITH EXTREME OIL AVOID THE TEMPTATION TO USE POWER
- MOVE YOUR FEET FIRST BEFORE MAKING ANY OTHER ADJUSTMENT
- MAKE A CHANGE WITH BOWLING BALLS WHEN YOU FEEL YOU'RE REALLY STRUGGLING AGAINST CONDITIONS

When I was a child, my parents emphasized the adage that people become smarter by keeping their eyes open and mouth shut. That advice paid off for me during a tournament in which I observed a bowler making notes after each game. After the block ended I asked about his note taking. He said that all lanes have individual characteristics and that by having a record of each lane he could exploit his strategic insights the next time he bowled on that particular pair.

The information that I can now call upon before bowling a game is absolutely vital to gaining a

game only to be faced with a split or a washout. You can then make the appropriate adjustment for the second frame only to discover that the right and left lanes of that pair are dissimilar.

That's why I always chart lanes. Had it not been for that habit I would not have won the 1990 Don Carter Classic in New Orleans. I earned the top seed for the stepladder format title round by just thirteen pins over Mike Edwards. On the show I defeated Mike in the championship game, 214 to 191.

greater margin for error on my shots, knowing I had an edge on the field increased my confidence. While the rest of the top twenty-four produced a composite average of 217.4, I managed to post a 227.6. That may sound like a big difference—and it is—but it comes down to only one extra hit per game.

I bet I know what you're thinking: Parker, that sounds great, but we all know that lane oil migrates so that the combination of bowling ball characteristics, ball speed, wrist position, release, and line that worked to perfection on one

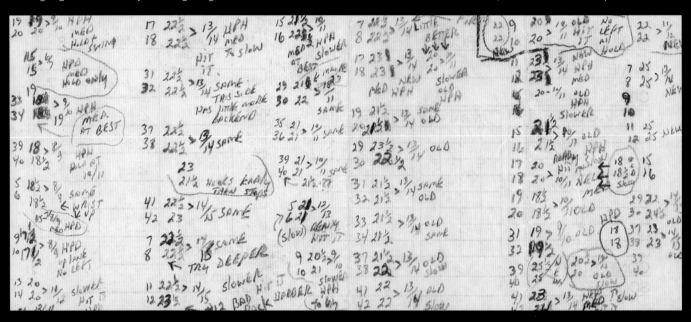

huge competitive edge on tour. Under our format, we are granted warm-up shots only prior to the start of each block. After every game we move to a new pair. Unlike with golf where players know each new hole's yardage and can see hazards like sand traps and ponds, all bowling lanes appear to be the same. But looks are deceiving. Every top player on the PBA and PWBA tours can repeat shots and string strikes. Thus, a very big part of being a successful pro is one's ability to get lined up on a new pair a frame or two quicker than does the competition. You can throw a "perfect" shot in the first frame of a new

I played about half of the pairs near the gutter and the remainder from inside while aiming around or just inside of the second arrow. Throughout the qualifying segment of that tournament I discovered which line worked better on every lane based solely on trial and error. During match play when I returned to a pair I was able to start every game with an educated guess as to where it was best to play. Nine times out of ten I was right. Thus, instead of bowling two good games and then donating a game I was able, at worst, to sacrifice only a frame or two. Not only did that provide me with a better reaction and a

time could be useless even a game or two later. You're right.

However, lane traits tend to be consistent. Let's say that the left lane of a pair hooks two boards more than the right lane when there is a lot of oil that makes them tight. Even when they become dry and begin to hook a lot you can bet that the left lane will hook proportionately more. It could be two boards or, perhaps one or three. But "reading" the results of my first shot on one lane should provide a pretty good clue about where and how to play the other. I also know how a certain pair or portion of the house compares to another. For example, many centers were constructed incrementally. Known as "split" houses, they were first built with a certain number of lanes and later expanded. The new series of lanes might hook more or less than the originals. Best of all, my handwriting is so awful that my notes look like some sort of encrypted nuclear submarine secrets during wartime. There can't possibly be another bowler who could ever make head or tails out of my scribbling. Had it been legible, here is the type of information they could have uncovered for every lane:

on a tight lane, "Slow and get the ball into an early roll.").

11. How I fared that game.

12. Where my strike ball made contact with the pins.

13. Which pins remain standing.

14. How the conversion shot went.

I also keep track of how many left-handers have rolled on those lanes since I was last there. This lets me know if I should expect a left-hander track to be worn into the oil on that lane. Even factors beyond my control are noted. For exam-

ciously save the two permissible reracks per game for a key shot such as late in the game or when I'm on a string of strikes. Knowing that one lane tends to yield a tight rack will allow me to avoid the pitfall of wasting a rerack in the second frame after having spared in the first frame.

Using my charts to see how specific balls perform comes in handy. It allows me to see when a ball needs to be traded in for a new one. I go through upward of one hundred balls annually. Just as a tire's tread suffers minor wear and tear due to the friction between it and the road, all

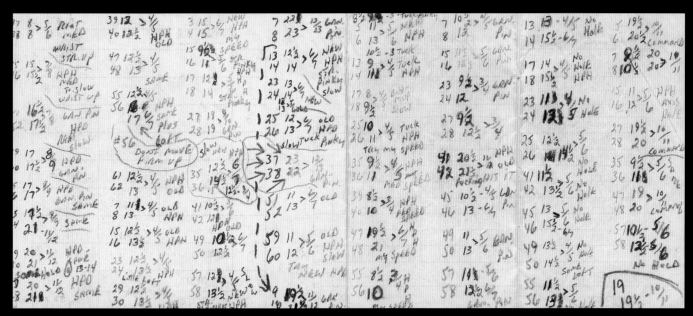

1. The board on which I stand for my strike shot.

2. My aiming point (the board number and how far down the lane—that is, what strike line).

3. What ball I used (including surface type and drilling specifications).

4. My hand position.

5. Approximate ball speed.

6. Whether or not my small finger was tucked.

7. How much, if any, I was lofting my shots.

8. Any miscellaneous information about each lane's characteristics/tendencies.

9. The nature of the racks on each lane.

10. Any keys to success (I might write to myself

ple, let's say that the rack on the left lane tends to be poor with the pocket too tight. Knowing that the 2-pin (for us left-handers) or the 3-pin (right-handed players) is slightly too close to the headpin could result in a lot of weak hits on good shots. For me, that could mean a 7-pin leave rather than a strike. So what good does it do to make a note of something that I would notice prior to each delivery? First, I'm mentally prepared for what could be a challenging game. If I know that the fifth game of a block is on such a pair I will enter that game determined not to become unnerved. More importantly, I will judi-

bowling balls absorb lane conditioner (oil). At my level, even a minor amount of oil soaking, which slightly alters a ball's reaction, will make a difference. Just as a race car driver's pit crew changes tires at the first hint of tread loss, I will drill a new ball when the one I've been using takes on any appreciable amount of oil.

T here are a lot of enjoyable ways to spend a Thursday or a Friday night in Dallas, Texas. But when I was there for the 1999 Don Carter PBA Classic Tournament and had made only one trip to the pay window during my first three tournaments of that year, I had absolutely no interest in taking in a sporting event or a movie, or going shopping. Instead, I spent several hours working on my game. I got started at about ten o'clock, long after the fans had left Don Carter's All-Star Lanes. That seemed like a good idea at the time, given that my earnings at that point ($1,155) covered only about one-third of my expenses.

I realized that the new oil pattern meant that I would have to decrease my ball speed to increase my carry. So I was on the lanes well past midnight on both Thursday and Friday. I achieved a lower speed by holding the ball lower during my stance, walking to the line at a slower pace, and decreasing the tempo of all of my movements. I focused on rolling the ball off my hand in such a manner as to get it into the perfect skid-roll-hook pattern, since I had noticed that my shots had far too much skid and precious little hook.

The next week in Austin I used only a little of what I had practiced in Dallas. But I sincerely believe that those late-night marathon sessions enabled me to get just enough extra pins to qualify for match play, make the TV show, and subsequently defeat Jason Couch, Patrick Healey Jr., and Pete Weber during the title round. That marked the first of three consecutive events in which I reached the championship round en route to the best year of my career up to that point. Those late-night practice sessions were key to my achievements.

DESIGNING A PRACTICE SESSION

As with anything worthwhile in life, becoming a better bowler takes a lot of work. But hard work, in and of itself, isn't sufficient. Hard work isn't necessarily its own reward. The hardest-working athlete in all of sports is a bull. It can always be counted upon to fight with every ounce of all-out effort until its last dying breath. But it almost always loses because of the matador's vastly superior ability to think. To bowl for hours on end without a plan is to be like the bull. For your practice to achieve its mission three components must be present: a theme, a plan, and an execution.

First, have a theme, an objective. By being analytical as you are competing you will have observed areas of your game that require the most improvement. Pick the most urgent of those and design a session to focus exclusively on that component. My practice mantra is: one session, one mission.

Your theme having been identified, you now need a plan. For example, say your problem is rolling strikes when the oil on the lanes starts to break down and your favorite line no longer is working. Your plan might then be to play the dots game (see page 142).

Finally, execute your plan, taking care that you do not confuse quantity for quality. The noted British soccer coach Charles Hughes is right when he declares that practice doesn't make perfect, practice makes permanent. If the amount of time you bowl exceeds the length of your attention span you will get sloppy. All that you will have "achieved" is to hone bad habits. I practice only for as long as I am able to give one hundred percent on every delivery.

I want to be able to duplicate the various components of my delivery and to be able to do so while changing speeds, strike lines, wrist positions, and releases. With anything that you practice, remember that the key to success lies in your ability to repeat. To add a trick to your arsenal is a positive, but not if it's at the expense of picking up a new problem. For example, there are times when it pays to loft your shots to minimize the effects of the head portion of the lanes. But if lofting causes you to lose balance or sacrifice your timing, you will find that your game will suffer.

There are two more common pitfalls you should avoid: don't be the player who just bowls practice games for score, nor the one who attempts only to throw strike shots and hits the reset button if any wood is left standing. That's not to say that it isn't okay to do either on occasion, but if one of these descriptions fits all of your practices you aren't likely to experience much improvement.

In my opinion, at least ninety percent of league players undervalue the significance of filling frames. Even if your strike ball is weak, you can still average above a 180 if you are able to keep the ball in play and consistently convert spares. Improving your ability to do so is the quickest and surest way to jump-start your scores. For most players, that means upgrading accuracy. Learning to throw the ball dead straight at spares doesn't come easily, especially if your strike shot tends to hook a lot. There is no great secret to this, other than to review the skills section in this book, and then to spend ample time practicing this vital aspect of the sport.

After you're able to roll relatively straight at your spares, try this challenge: do so while using your soft-shell strike ball. This will force you to keep your

IN PRACTICE SESSIONS, DON'T JUST AUTOMATICALLY HIT THE RESET BUTTON IF WOOD IS LEFT STANDING; ROLL YOUR CONVERSION SHOT.

- IDENTIFY A SPECIFIC OBJECTIVE FOR EACH SESSION
- DEVELOP A CLEAR PLAN TO REACH YOUR OBJECTIVE
- DON'T INGRAIN BAD HABITS THROUGH SLOPPY PRACTICE
- DON'T IGNORE THE STRAIGHT SPARE SHOT IN YOUR SESSIONS

COMPARE YOUR GOOD SHOTS WITH YOUR BAD ONES ON VIDEOTAPE.

- KEEP A RECORD OF YOUR MATCH FRAMES TO IDENTIFY PROBLEM AREAS

- USE A COMPUTER TO UNCOVER PATTERNS IN YOUR PLAY

- VIDEOTAPE YOUR SESSIONS TO SEE FLAWS

- ENLIST THE HELP OF COACHES OR FRIENDS TO OBSERVE YOUR DELIVERY

ABOVE LEFT: WITH OVER ONE MILLION DOLLARS IN CAREER EARNINGS, ALETA SILL IS ONE OF THE MOST SUCCESSFUL PWBA PLAYERS TODAY. *ABOVE RIGHT:* CAROLYN DORIN-BALLARD IS AN UP-AND-COMING PWBA PLAYER.

wrist flat and your hand behind the ball. Any minor flaw will be magnified when your shot hits the dry portion of the lane.

PINPOINTING PROBLEMS

A key part of designing a practice session is pinpointing your main problems. Are you failing to carry shots in the pocket? Are you missing an inordinate number of spares? Are you unable to roll consecutive strike balls over the same target? Do you bowl one great game only to come crashing down to earth in the subsequent contest?

One sure way to help identify a con-

cern is to produce a written record of all of your shots. (See pages 134–35 for a detailed explanation of the charts I keep during every PBA event.) You should note the following data after each frame: where your strike ball made contact with the pins (right of the pocket, light, pocket, high flush, nose, Brooklyn, or left of the pocket) and what pins, if any, remained standing. Also, what happened on your conversion attempt? (If you failed to fill the frame, write down what was wrong with your second ball.)

When the round is over you can utilize modern technology (that is, a computer) to create a permanent record of your performance. Note your strike per-

centage and how many shots fell into each category. Say you find, for example, that you struck on eleven of thirty-one shots but that you hit the pocket on only fourteen occasions. Obviously, your lack of accuracy is a concern. Conversely, had you hit the pocket twenty-five times but carried only eleven shots it may be time for an equipment change, or you might consider altering your strike line or working on imparting a more powerful release.

One of today's greatest tools for upping your scores can be found in your den. The VCR is one of my best coaches.

Of course, I have the advantage of being able to study any of the well over one hundred games that I've rolled on television. But you don't have to be a touring pro to have a friend tape you during practice.

The most instructive camera angles are from behind or from the same side as your bowling hand. If you are like the typical bowler, you might not realize that you are dropping your shoulder or taking two steps before putting the ball in motion, throwing your timing out of kilter. Perhaps there's a bump in your armswing. By comparing good to bad shots you will probably discover a common flaw or two that can be easily

BEING ABLE TO
REPEAT THE SAME
SERIES OF MOTIONS
SHOULD BE A
CONSTANT GOAL
DURING PRACTICE.

If I could point my finger at any one asset that has allowed me to succeed for a prolonged period of time on the PBA tour it would be my versatility. Although lane conditions and equipment have evolved considerably since my rookie year of 1970, I have still been able to compete with consistent success. Every bowler, including the pros, has a favorite line. The vast majority of the players who are full-time touring pros have the capability of winning a tournament when the conditions allow them to play their so-called A-game. However, the factor that separates the genuine stars from the pack is that the world-class bowler can win when the conditions aren't conducive to his or her preferred strike line. I take the greatest pride in the events that I have won while playing my B-game against a rival who was able to play his A-game. Becoming a versatile player takes talent married to hard work.

The main way to become more versatile is through practice, and my favorite practice activity is known as the dots game. Here's how it works. Using only your strike ball, stand on the fifth board. From that angle, attempt to strike. After you have hit the pocket on four consecutive shots or doubled (your choice), your feet move five boards inward. Once again, strive to reach your goal (a predesignated number of successive pocket hits or strikes). When you've succeeded, move another five boards. Continue until you're playing a deep inside line with your feet starting on the thirty-fifth board. Then work your way back to where you began.

If you are a high-level player whose average is on the happy side of 200 you can make the game even more challenging. I once read that, when he played at Princeton and later with the New York Knickerbockers, Bill Bradley didn't leave practice until he had sunk twenty-five straight free-throws. If he made twenty-four straight but missed number twenty-five he would start all over until he reached his quota. Similarly, when playing the dots game you have to return to your starting point if you miss the pocket entirely. Don't go home until you have covered the entire approach successfully—or until the night cleaning crew throws you out!

While this game is aimed at top-of-the-line players, it can be played by anyone. With each move you will find that you have to make physical adjustments. As a general rule, when you are playing up the boards (standing far right for a right-handed player and vice versa for a lefty), a good amount of speed is required to keep the shot on line. Conversely, when deep inside, you will need to impart more revs (revolutions). That will mean a cupped wrist, probably a decrease in ball speed, and maximum lift at the point of release.

Normally, when I move far to my left (I'm a right-hander) changing balls proves helpful. However, the purpose of the dots game is to provide you with the maximum challenge. By keeping the same ball for all angles you will put the versatility of your physical game to the fullest test.

remedied through practice.

Equally helpful is to work with a qualified instructor over a prolonged period of time. Even if it's not a professional coach, a watchful eye will be helpful. For instance, my wife Leslie was an outstanding intercollegiate bowler in her own right and she knows my game as well—or better—than do I. She can pick up the most subtle of mistakes. My mom, although she is not an expert on the game, has seen me bowl since I was ten, and she doesn't hesitate to tell me when something doesn't look quite right to her. The primary responsibility of my ball reps, Art McKee and Rich Benoit, is to watch my ball reaction and tell me if and what equipment change might prove advantageous. They, too, also have keen eyes for detail and have helped me to correct technical flaws in my delivery.

I don't know of any pro on either tour who doesn't rely upon a coach (or coaches) for at least occasional assistance. You should too. There are literally thousands of PBA and PWBA members nationwide. A considerable percentage of them are teaching pros. Don't be shy about approaching one of them to take a series of lessons.

Sometimes your problem areas may be caused by a lack of muscle tone or physical coordination. The best way to correct this is through a regular fitness regimen. Although bowling doesn't have the aerobic demands of other sports, staying fit helps you bowl better. Yes, we all know that there are bowlers—even some of my fellow pros—who don't exactly look like athletes. It is possible to be overweight or smoke cigarettes and still bowl well. Nevertheless, I firmly believe that it is not possible to be overweight or smoke cigarettes and bowl your best week in and week out. This is especially true during longer-format tournament play.

Your role models should be Amleto Monacelli, Kim Adler, and Kim Terrell. Each is every bit as fit as virtually any pro in any other sport. In fact, Amleto's discipline in adhering to an exhausting regi-

men—he runs almost every morning—has provided him with a great competitive advantage. Kim Adler is an absolute fanatic when it comes to fitness. When she isn't competing on the lanes she can usually be found mountain biking, rock climbing, or snowboarding.

I have been on tour full-time since 1985. While I am certainly no longer twenty-one years old, my weight today is only slightly higher than it was then. I defy anyone to name a top PBA performer who has enjoyed long-term success during the past decade and is also overweight. For health and bowling reasons you should eat right, pay attention to how many calories you consume, and

get enough sleep.

A fitness routine should complement your regular practice sessions. However, this takes up a huge chunk of time and the reality of the twenty-first century is that time is of the essence. Trying to balance work, family, and recreation is no easy trick for most people. In all likelihood, you have only a finite amount of time to practice. That's why it is imperative that any extra moments you can spend on the lane be as productive as possible. How much you are able to practice will never be as important as how well you practice.

ABOVE: FORMER PLAYER OF THE YEAR AND 1999 U.S. OPEN CHAMPION KIM ADLER IS ALSO AN AVID ROCK CLIMBER, MOUNTAIN BIKER, AND SNOWBOARDER. MAINTAINING SUCH A HIGH LEVEL OF OVERALL FITNESS IMPROVES HER GAME TREMENDOUSLY.

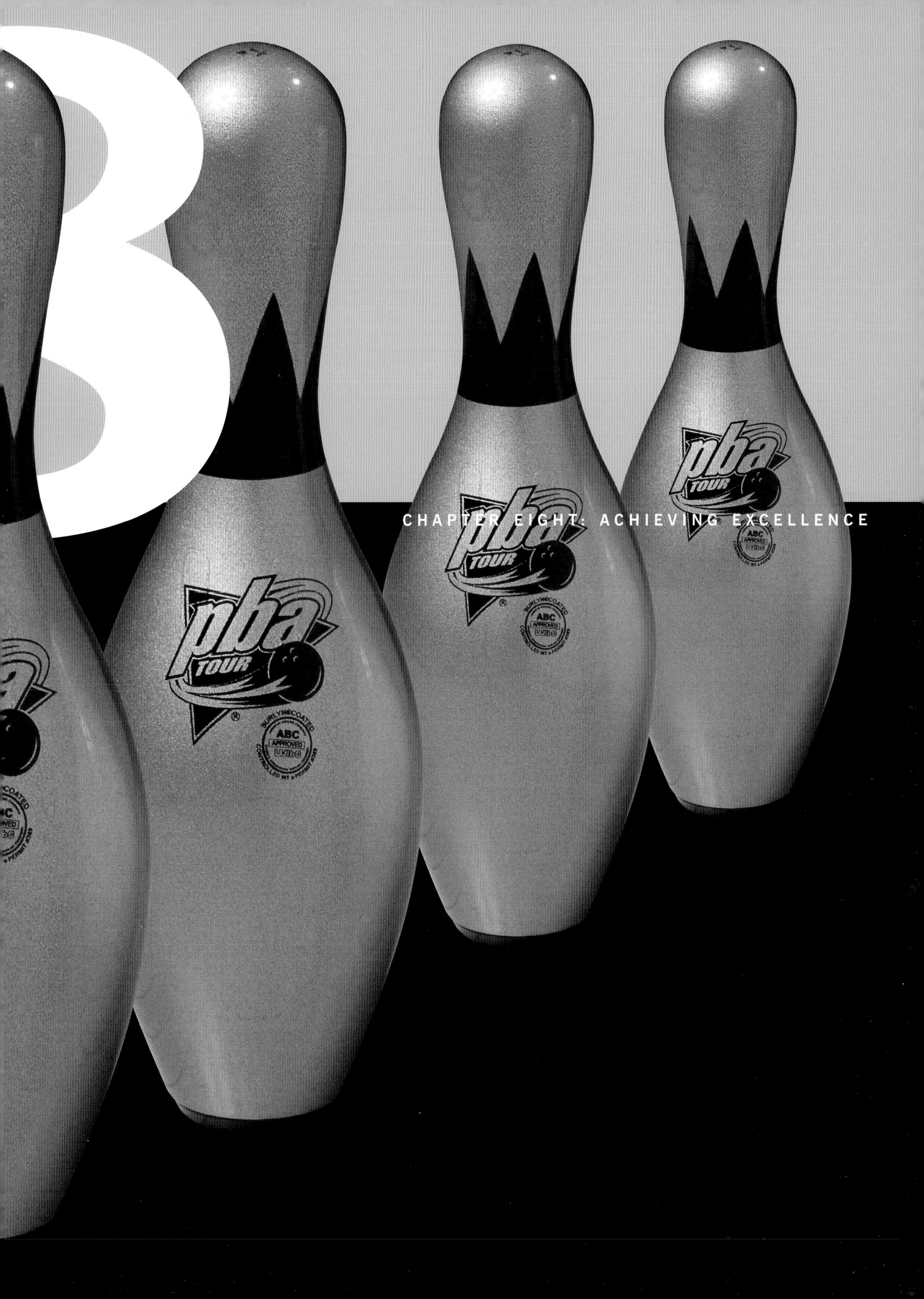

CHAPTER EIGHT: ACHIEVING EXCELLENCE

Most of America's tens of millions of participants consider bowling to be a grand hobby that provides recreation, fun, exercise, and an evening out with good friends. While smaller in number, there are also a lot of people for whom bowling is the sport of choice. Those of us in that category possess a keen desire to test our mettle at the highest possible level our abilities will permit.

Achieving excellence is never easy in any endeavor. It is, however, an enormously rewarding experience for those who succeed. Perhaps your goal is to take me on at the professional level, to break the bank at a megabucks tournament, to represent your country by proudly donning a Team USA shirt, or to defray the costs of your college education by earning scholarship dollars. All of the above requires a lot of talent and dedication, along with a reasonable amount of good fortune. When people ask my advice, I tell them to go for it. There is no dishonor in falling short of a goal if you've given it your best shot.

WICHITA STATE UNIVERSITY TEAM MEMBERS CHERISHING THEIR TRIUMPH IN THE 1998 IBC (INTER-COLLEGIATE BOWLING CHAMPIONSHIP)

- TAKE ADVANTAGE OF THE INCREASING NUMBER OF BOWLING SCHOLARSHIPS OFFERED

- CHOOSE A TEAM THAT WILL CHALLENGE YOU

- BE PREPARED TO DEAL WITH A SCHEDULE HEAVY WITH TIME CONSTRAINTS

MAJOR BOWLING ORGANIZATIONS

- PBA (PROFESSIONAL BOWLERS ASSOCIATION)

- PWBA (PROFESSIONAL WOMEN'S BOWLERS ASSOCIATION)

- ABC (AMERICAN BOWLING CONGRESS)

- WIBC (WOMEN'S INTERNATIONAL BOWLING CONGRESS)

- YABA (YOUNG AMERICAN BOWLING ALLIANCE)

- BPAA (BOWLING PROPRIETORS' ASSOCIATION OF AMERICA)

- USAB (USA BOWLING)

- CBUSA (COLLEGE BOWLING USA)

- COMPETING ABROAD BETTERS YOUR GAME BY EXPOSING YOU TO NEW CONDITIONS

- TRAIN FOR QUICK, INTENSIVE QUALIFYING ROUNDS

- FOCUS ON YOUR STRIKE BALL MORE THAN YOUR SPARE

A BOWLING EDUCATION

While I hit the road to pursue fame and fortune at an early age, more and more top-level junior bowlers are now opting to attend college. There are considerable scholarship dollars available, particularly for female players, thanks to Title IX (federal legislation that mandates gender-equitable athletic opportunities).

There are also countless youth tournaments, both scratch and handicap, where the prizes are scholarship dollars placed in escrow and earmarked for college tuition. I recommend that a serious youth player enter as many of those as possible. Not only are the potential economic benefits considerable, the player will be exposed to bowling in different centers on a wide range of lane conditions.

Picking the right college is never easy. You're selecting an institution whose intellectual demands and offerings must match your needs and capabilities as well as a place that will serve as your home for four years. Additionally, you are looking for a program with a knowledgeable and dedicated coach, satisfactory facilities, and a demanding schedule. Gathering this key information can be done by visiting campus while school is in session. Ask questions of those on the team. Don't be shy about compiling personal references. And, of course, the cost of tuition plus room and board must be weighed.

You want to make sure that you start at a college where you will be challenged—both in the classroom and on the lanes. Remember that sometimes it's more rewarding to join a team where you will not be a lead player. This ensures that you will be challenged. Another consideration is the team's commitment to academic performance. The bowling program at Wichita State, for example, is known for giving equal amount of weight to academic and athletic activities. The head coach there, Gordon Vadakin, says he values well-rounded student athletes because they turn out to be the best players. He believes a strong academic regimen teaches the ability to organize and prioritize one's goals, which applies equally well on the lanes.

Make no mistake about it, the time demands of intercollegiate bowling are considerable. Travel to weekend tournaments is often over long distances. To stay ahead of the pack academically isn't easy. To earn a degree in four years, some students may end up having to attend summer school every year.

One must also be patient. Long before they became prominent players on the PBA tour, Patrick Healey Jr. and Chris Barnes had to bide their time at WSU. In a program that attracted the nation's finest scholastic bowlers, neither was able to earn a roster spot on the first team as a freshman. However, each was sufficiently mature to understand that his long-term interests were better served by being a small fish in a big pond than vice versa.

BIG-TIME AMATEUR PLAY

For several years now, the caliber and sophistication of the top rookies on our tour has been very impressive. Much of that is attributable to collegiate bowling and Team USA. In any sport, there is no greater honor than representing your country. With all of the millions of dollars that tennis players can earn, the top stars will tell you that they are never under more pressure than when competing in the Davis Cup. Ditto for golfers and the Ryder Cup. And that certainly applies to us bowlers in the Reichert Cup (named for the former Brunswick CEO who has been a driving force at promoting international play). Aside from the thrill of such competition, there is the tangible benefit of learning how to adjust to different time zones, cultures, climates, and, on occasion, vastly different lane conditions.

Another route is the megabucks circuit. A successful player at that level must have ice water running through his veins, considering some of the incredible prizes to be won—and the structure of the prize funds are exceedingly top-heavy. To prepare for such events it is important to contemplate their format. Most of them involve short qualifying rounds followed by head-to-head play over a game or two. Thus, it's a sprint in which the ability to get lined up quickly is essential. Contrast that to the PBA tour, where a player requires greater long-term focus. PBA players must normally roll forty-two games or more just to qualify for the title round. If a PBA tournament is like a twelve-round title fight, then a megabucks event is equivalent to a three-round amateur bout in which wild punches are constantly being thrown at a frenetic pace.

If I were to have gone the megabucks route I would have prepared by practicing on my ability to throw strikes from every angle. Sure, filling frames still counts, so you don't want to squander easy spare-conversion opportunities. However, being solid and consistent usually isn't the ticket to the big money. I would arrive at the center early to discover what balls and strike lines seemed to be working the best. If I struggled at all during the warm-up I would not hesitate to make a radical change. In that respect, it is not dissimilar to a televised PBA championship round, where the stakes for strikes are high on every shot.

TURNING PRO

To become a PWBA member you must maintain a sanctioned league average over a minimum of sixty-six games for each of two consecutive seasons with an average of at least 190 (for national membership) or 180 (regional). Alternatively, you must, according to PWBA literature, "demonstrate the ability to perform at that level or show cause why you were unable to do so." Also required is a copy of your birth certificate to prove that you were born a female, a completed application form, a current professional portrait photo, and a dues payment.

To be accepted into the PBA a player must be at least eighteen years old or a high-school graduate (a nineteen-year-old without his diploma needs a letter of consent from a parent or guardian). The player must have carried no less than a 200 average for sixty-six or more games during the two most recent successive sanctioned league seasons or 220 for the most recent season. Also required is legal proof of birthdate and the initiation fee. It is requested that, if available, an action photograph be included. All of that is mailed to the PBA's national headquarters. After acceptance, dues are owed.

To apply is one thing. To win money is entirely a different matter. The majority of players who try the tour quickly earn the label of a donor. For every superstar you see being handed a big check on national television there are two-thirds of that week's field whose entry fees helped to pay the winner.

When I joined the tour graduating from PBA School was mandatory. I attended it in San Antonio. One of our lecturers was the great Carmen Salvino. A true legend, he spelled out the realities of life on the road. Carmen acknowledged the many temptations and pitfalls to avoid. The essence of his message: you are crazy if you think that you can chase ladies, drink, stay up half of the night, and then get up to beat the best players in the world.

Carmen was right. I soon discovered that the biggest enemy on tour is boredom. There is a lot of dead time between squads, especially when failing to qualify for match play. I make a concerted effort to pass my time constructively. A relaxing dinner at a nice restaurant with a few friends beats gobbling down fast-food. Catching a decent movie is preferable to lying in one's hotel room bed and staring for hours at the same four walls. Watching my fellow bowlers compete to see if I can learn anything is a better alternative than inhaling thick air in a smoke-filled lounge.

In anything you do, your attitude will determine if you will fulfill your potential. One key factor in my consistent success in the Japan Cup is that I

- REMEMBER THAT A COMMITMENT TO TRAVEL IS NECESSARY

- YOU NEED TO MAINTAIN A HEALTHY LIFESTYLE

- A SERIOUS ATTITUDE TOWARD THE SPORT IS ESSENTIAL TODAY

ABOVE: MANY PROFESSIONAL STARS SUCH AS PATRICK HEALEY JR. ARE PRODUCTS OF THE BOWLING PROGRAM AT WICHITA STATE UNIVERSITY.

1 VIRGINIA BEACH **Brunswick** VIRGINIA BEACH 2

Brunswick

ARENA BOWLING PRO-
VIDES A GREAT FAN
ATMOSPHERE WHILE
TESTING THE ABILITY
OF THE COMPETITORS
TO FULLY FOCUS ON
THE TASK AT HAND.

truly enjoy experiencing new and different things. I have found that the Japanese bowlers welcome us with open arms. Too many of us sheltered Americans travel abroad and complain about tiny inconveniences. Instead of moaning about the cost of a hamburger in Tokyo, I tried sushi and found several varieties to my liking. In anything I do I always seek out the positives and try to ignore any negatives. I find that people with negative attitudes only

The vast majority of modern competitive bowlers see themselves as serious athletes and behave accordingly. Moreover, the "retro" types who aren't fit might win some events and money but they could all do better with better habits.

One final word: whenever you are on the lanes always give every shot all that you have. Don't get angry or become psychologically shattered when it's clear you aren't going to prevail. Treat every upcoming delivery as a potential learning

hurt themselves.

I have often heard it said that achieving success is a choice that one makes. To be certain, all of us are born with different levels of innate ability. That's why, to me, success is defined as making the most of your potential. Whether you're a fifteen-year-old aspiring to earn money for college or a top pro striving for the Hall of Fame, the choices that you make will have a major impact on whether or not you reach your goals.

I am not suggesting that every top player is a saint. Bowling lore is filled with tales of characters who thrived in competition but weren't exactly society's top role models. But such bowlers are fewer and farther between nowadays.

experience. Prove to yourself that you have the guts to compete to your fullest no matter what the circumstances. To do any less is to shortchange yourself and the great sport of bowling.

ABOVE FROM LEFT:
THE REICHERT CUP IS BOWLING'S EQUIVA-LENT OF TENNIS'S DAVIS CUP OR GOLF'S RYDER CUP; TEAM USA, WHICH REPRE-SENTS THE COUNTRY IN INTERNATIONAL COMPETITIONS, IS AN ALL-STAR LINEUP OF TOP NONPROFES-SIONAL PLAYERS.

It has often been written of me that I was among the best-prepared newcomers in the history of the PBA tour. I consider it a great honor to have won the 1998 Harry Golden Award for Rookie of the Year. While most first-year pros serve a painful and financially draining apprenticeship, I was able to place twenty-sixth in earnings. Very few of the sport's most accomplished stars in the annals of the tour enjoyed that much success so early in their careers. The following year I captured my first two PBA titles. Only Parker and Jason Couch ended 1999 listed above me on the IRS's hit list. The credit for my having been able to enjoy a relatively smooth transition into the pro ranks has a lot to do with the experiences I gained through intercollegiate bowling, with Team USA, and on the big-bucks so-called amateur circuit. I strongly advise any youngster with big-time bowling aspirations to consider emulating the route I took.

We are all products of our environments. The outstanding environment provided by a first-class intercollegiate bowling program with great coaching makes you a better bowler. Of equal significance, the academic and social demands will help to make you a more interesting, developed individual. Having a diploma is a great safety net. I'm also better able to handle finances. Even the courses whose content was not relevant to my occupation today were beneficial as they taught me, among other things, how to meet deadlines.

When I arrived at Wichita State I was probably viewed as being talented but extremely raw. I was athletic and could hook the whole lane but I couldn't make a spare and I lacked any appreciable tools. I certainly wasn't very astute at strategy. The WSU program operated on a straight qualifying system for their three squads. As a freshman I placed fifteenth—I was the last guy on the last team!

Luckily for me, Pat Henry was our C-team coach and Dan Dick was my roommate. Despite marathon practices with them, my college days were filled with highs and lows. As a sophomore I earned All-American recognition but then fell short of making the A-team the following year. Failing to qualify for the first unit that year was a bitter pill to swallow, but I had to admit that there was nobody to blame but myself. I'd been issued a challenge to improve. Then, though I was on our B-squad, I managed to win the ACU-I national title as a junior.

Between my junior and senior years I traveled to Atlanta in an attempt to earn a roster spot with Team USA. I finished tenth. My hopes of making it in 1992 ended in an automobile accident. The vehicle in which I was traveling rolled over. My bowling elbow met a windshield and ended up forty stitches the worse for wear. Not being able to bend one's elbow makes rolling shots a bit problematic. Finally, I broke through in 1993 in Akron, Ohio. It was great to compete in such places as Thailand and Malaysia while representing our country. From a bowling standpoint, I was exposed to new lane conditions and to facing players with differing approaches to the sport. Exceptional coaches like Fred Borden and Jeri Edwards added further refinements to my game. Finally I made the transformation to a legitimate bowler. By my mid-twenties I was a far cry from the kid who had arrived at college with a real high backswing and yahoo at the foul line.

During my four years with Team USA I also entered several high-roller "amateur" tournaments. The highlight of my megabucks career was winning back-to-back sweepers in Las Vegas during a single weekend in 1994. I walked away with over sixty thousand dollars. Under those formats a player is regularly exposed to having to strike in the tenth frame with a lot of green on the line. I learned how to deal with pressure, which was a great lesson for tour events in which an entire week's fate can often be determined by the results of a single delivery.

I'm thankful that I took my lumps in college and with Team USA at an age when some guys were getting their heads handed to them on the tour. It's far less expensive to bowl a bad game for your school team than when the money for your next meal is at stake. If there's one point I'd like to emphasize, it's that the road hasn't always been smooth. The positive thinking of my collegiate coaches and teammates helped ease the pain of the defeats. I learned that what ultimately separates stars from also-rans is that successful people are sufficiently motivated that a loss serves as a spur that drives them to work harder. I know that missing the A-team as a junior led to ample self-reflection and many late nights working on my game. Had it not been for that, I probably wouldn't be where I am today.

The Straight Shot for Spares and Splits: Where to Release and Aim Your Ball

HAND	LEAVE	BALL RELEASE BOARD	TARGET BOARD / ARROW
Right	7	13	20 / 4th (center)
Left	7	27	20 / 4th (center)
Right	4	17	20 / 4th (center)
Left	4	18	15 / 3rd
Right	2-7	17	20 / 4th (center)
Left	2-7	17	15 / 3rd
Right	3-10	24	20 / 4th (center)
Left	3-10	4	11 / Just inside 2nd
Right	2-8	18	20 / 4th (center)
Left	2-8	16	15 / 3rd
Right	3-9	22	20 / 4th (center)
Left	3-9	4	10 / 2nd
Right	10	26	20 / 4th (center)
Left	10	4	12/13 / 2nd/3rd
Right	6	24	20 / 4th (center)
Left	6	4	11 / Just inside 2nd
Right	2	18	20 / 4th (center)
Left	2	16	15 / 3rd
Right	3	22	20 / 4th (center)
Left	3	4	10 / 2nd
Right	4-7-10	15	20 / 4th (center)
Left	4-7-10	25	20 / 4th (center)
Right	6-7-10	27	20 / 4th (center)
Left	6-7-10	4	13 / 2nd/3rd
Right	1-2-4-10	27	25 / 5th
Left	1-3-6-7	6	10 / 2nd
Right	2-4-5-8	19	20 / 4th
Left	3-5-6-9	4	9th / 2nd

The Strike Line Split Shot: How to Make Adjustments off Your Strike Line

HAND	LEAVE	DIRECTION TO MOVE	SUGGESTED BOARDS TO MOVE
Right	5-7	Left	2/3
Left	5-10	Right	3
Right	3-6-9-10	Left	4
Left	2-4-7-8	Right	4

EVENT	PROBLEM	SOLUTION	RESULT
1989 Brunswick World Open	Lanes excessively hooking with shots breaking prematurely. Every few shots one went high	Untucked pinkie finger so ball would go farther down the lane and hold the line to the pocket	Won the tournament
1999 ABC Masters	Lanes get progressively more tight as tournament unfolded. Every few shots a ball was missing light	Decreased ball speed by holding ball lower during address after having moved up on the approach	Qualified for the title round as the top seed
1999 Oronamin C Japan Cup	Shots occasionally hooking so faced with several multiple-pin spare combinations	Focused on "feeling" ring finger on the ball more than the middle to get ball farther down	Won the tournament
1998 Greater Detroit Open	Lanes so broken down that lefties were playing deep inside and most righties around second arrow	Moved farther inside to near fourth arrow to get more early oil	Week's top pinfall and won event with a 290 in championship game
2000 PBA National Championship	Extremely early hook with the ball hardly breaking once it got past the arrows. Entire field suffered	Rather than fight condition, opted for a suitcase release with a relatively straight line to the pocket	Made late charge to just miss TV finals
1990 Don Carter Classic	Thumb was so excessively swollen due to hot and humid weather that couldn't exit ball cleanly	Placed tissue over thumb hole and inserted thumb into the ball occasionally	Won the tournament
1997 Showboat Invitational	Slippery approaches on synthetic lanes compromised vital balance during release	Wiped sliding shoe before every shot with a towel. Before next game cleaned with Scotch Brite	Won the tournament
1992 PBA Doubles Classic	Extremely humid Texas weather caused foot to stick at the foul line	Changed disk on bottom of sliding foot to Teflon	Won the event with partner Hugh Miller
1997 Oronamin C Japan Cup	Carried well but not nearly as well as rivals on extremely high-scoring condition	Changed to a ball with different hooking characteristics while moved slightly deeper inside	Qualified first for finals with 23-9 match play record and 239.4 average

PARKER BOHN III was the preeminent left-handed bowler during the nineties. As of 2000, only three players were ahead of him for official career earnings and only seven men had exceeded his twenty-two career national tour titles. Nine times in the ten-year span that began in 1990 he finished among the top ten in official earnings, including five years during which he paced all southpaws in that category.

Bohn saved the best for last, running away with the balloting for the 1999 Chris Schenkel PBA Player of the Year Award. His 228.04 average easily broke Walter Ray Williams Jr.'s record.

In February of 1999 he captured the Columbia 300 Open in Austin, Texas, by defeating Pete Weber, 225–211. Win number two that year came in the Albany suburb of Latham, New York, during the Empire State Open in April. Career title number twenty resulted after running away with a sizzling 241.8 average over fifty-six games at Las Vegas's Showboat Hotel, Casino & Bowling Center. The trophy was lifted following a 241–220 conquest of Amleto Monacelli.

Not content to dominate in North America, Bohn set another standard during an Asian excursion in September of 1999. Earning one of the sixteen places that are reserved for the PBA's point leaders, he set out to capture an unprecedented third Oronamin C Japan Cup. Again qualifying on top at Tokyo Port Bowl thanks to a 229.2 average and a 19-12-1 match play ledger, Bohn faced Norm Duke for the $50,000 top prize. A thrilling 234–233 victory separated Bohn from two-time Japan Cup kings Monacelli and Pete Weber. In the process, Bohn also became the only bowler in that tournament's history to successfully defend his title.

Had there been any lingering doubts as to who would reign supreme in 1999, they were dispelled during October's Track/Dexter Open at Roseland Bowl in the Buffalo suburb of Canandaigua, New York. Top-seeded over second qualifier Monacelli, Bohn ended up facing incumbent Walter Ray Williams Jr. in the title game. A 274–246 result confirmed the passing of the torch.

As if five wins weren't sufficient, Bohn came within one shot of having captured the ABC Masters after having been the top seed entering the title round. He also paced the field over sixty-four games during the Bayer/Brunswick Touring Players Championship en route to a second place finish.

Nor was 1999 a fluke. The prior year Bohn came within an eyelash of top player recognition, thanks to four titles. The highlight of 1998 came during the semifinal stage of the ABC Masters in front of a huge crowd at Reno's National Bowling Stadium. Facing Chris Sand and Mike Mullin in the shootout game, Bohn calmly buried three pocket hits in the tenth frame to become the twelfth player in PBA history to have rolled a televised perfect game. The consummate class act who is as popular with the public as he is with his peers, Bohn is the only four-time recipient of the Steve Nagy Award, an annual honor that is bestowed by players on a colleague who has displayed the most exemplary professionalism and sportsmanship.

MIKE AULBY After his beloved Islanders won four straight Stanley Cups, Aulby completed the first Grand Slam with his win at the 1995 Brunswick World Tournament of Champions to complement his triumphs in the 1989 BPAA U.S. Open, the ABC Masters (1989, 1995, and 1998), and the PBA National Championship (1979, 1985). He made it a Super Slam by taking the Touring Players Championship in 1996. Aulby is the only PBA Rookie of the Year winner who later became a Player of the Year during the twentieth century.

CHRIS BARNES Barnes is among the tour's foremost stars who is one of a very few to have excelled during his first few years on the tour. The former Wichita State All-America's encore in 1999 after becoming the PBA's 1998 Rookie of the Year included winning the Flagship Open in Erie and the Oregon Open in Portland while finishing third on the money list.

DREW CAREY The star of the extremely popular ABC-TV show that bears his name is also the longtime host of *Whose Line Is It Anyway?* An avid bowler and great friend to the sport, he has rolled exhibition matches during several PBA events. Extremely generous, Carey has quietly championed several worthwhile charities.

CINDY COBURN-CARROLL A four-time WIBC All-America, the Buffalo native has been inducted into eight halls of fame including the Women's Professional Bowling Hall of Fame and that of the WIBC. Between 1979 and 1996 she won fifteen tour titles, including the 1992 WIBC Queens, plus nine regional events.

JOHNNY PETRAGLIA Inducted into the PBA Hall of Fame in 1982, Petraglia has won fourteen national tour titles. He is the second male bowler to have completed the triple crown: the Firestone Tournament of Champions (1971), BPAA U.S. Open (1977), and the PBA National Championship (1980) as well as having won the 1998 PBA Senior National Championship. His composure with a $100,000 bonus on the line while completing a televised perfect game against Walter Ray Williams Jr. during the 1994 PBA National Championship was remarkable.

MARK ROTH Truly one of bowling's all-time greats, as of press time Roth had won more times on the national tour (thirty-four) than any right-hander in PBA history. Voted PBA Player of the Year in 1977, 1978, 1979, and 1984, Roth led the tour in official earnings four times. His eight titles in 1978 is the all-time single-year standard. Roth almost single-handedly revolutionized the sport with the tremendous power that he was able to generate on his strike shots.

KIM TERRELL A superb stylist with a silk-smooth approach, Terrell has excelled at every level of the game. A former collegiate All-America, she captured the 1988 FIQ Youth World All-Events title during her stint on Team USA. The following year she was named the Ebonite Rookie of the Year winner and has twice received the Robby Award for exceptional professionalism both on and off the lanes.

TAMMY TURNER The PWBA's 1994 top rookie produced that tour's best average two years later. Before winning four national pro titles during the nineties she received All-America recognition at West Texas A & M and was named the 1993 Amateur Bowler of the Year.

Parker Bohn III would like to offer special thanks to the following:

My parents, Parker Jr., and Jean, for always being there when I need them; Parker IV and Evan for the incredible inspiration that only comes from a child's love; Leslie Beamish for her unbridled support, both on and off the lanes; the Brunswick staff members and my tour roommates, Jason Couch and Doug Kent, for all of their assistance with the manuscript; my prize bowling pupil and good friend, Drew Carey, whose spare shooting accuracy is not yet quite as sharp as his wit; Rick Messina and Sharon Martin for arranging the details for the introduction; Jerry Conner and Ron Pagut, my initial sponsors, for providing the opportunity of a lifetime; Dave and Joann Davis for taking such an interest in me and offering so much great coaching; Mark Roth for pointing me in the right direction; Johnny Petraglia for taking a fellow Metropolitan Area southpaw under his wing; the PBA, without whom I could never have pursued and fulfilled my boyhood dreams; Jim Dressel and Luby Publishing for generously contributing their encyclopedic knowledge and several photos; Jerry Baltz and the Bowling Hall of Fame for all of their help; the American Bowling Congress, whose overworked staff gives and gives and gives; Brunswick's fabulous ball reps Rick Benoit, Art McKee, and Ray Edwards for their fantastic expertise, support, and friendship throughout the years; J.T. McDonald and Bryan Collins for their championing this project and their ceaseless support of the sport; Joe Norris for his invaluable help with the history chapter as well as having made so much incredible bowling history during his career; the Feingold family at Howell Lanes for the countless hours of available practice time, your friendship, and your encouragement; Josh Hyde and Larry Stella—how you have dealt with your lifelong physical challenges with ceaseless grace and courage has inspired me and has always put professional bowling in its proper perspective; Charles Miers and Chris Steighner for their late hours and editorial expertise.

The editors would like to offer special thanks to the following:

Jonathan Davis at Kegel Company for help with oil pattern illustrations; Ray Edwards at Brunswick; Mort Luby Jr. and Jim Dressel of Bowlers Journal International for their generous assistance with image research; J.T. McDonald at Brunswick; Mark Miller at ABC; Chuck Pezzano; John Takacs; and Jason Winkler at Ackerman McQueen.

Dan Herbst would like to offer special thanks to the following:

My dad Joseph, stepmother Lois, and sister Diana, for being the great people they are; my wife Sandy and sons Larry and Colin for simply being the best.

Allsport (pp. 18–19)

American Bowling Congress (pp. 14, 15 top, 24 top left, 25 bottom, 33 top, 34, 60, 152 right)

Bowler's Journal International (pp. 20 bottom center and botttom, 23, 24 bottom, 26 bottom, 27, 30, 31, 35, 54, 77, 78, 126, 128, 130–131, 140, 143, 152 left, 153)

Brunswick Indoor Recreation Group (pp. 32, 33 bottom, 48–49, 56, 63, 66–67)

Simon Bruty/Any Chance Productions (pp. 36–37, 39 left, 40–41, 43–45, 57, 64, 69, 70–71, 80–81, 100–101, 118–119, 136–137, 141)

Curtis Publishing Company (p. 28)

International Bowling Museum and Hall of Fame, St. Louis, Missouri, USA (pp. 10–11, 15 bottom, 17, 20 top and top center, 21, 22, 24 top center and right, 25 top, 26 top, 29, 68)

Thomas J. Kaminski (p. 35)

The Kegel Company, Inc. (pp. 52–53)

John Mutrux (pp. 39 right, 65, 88–98, 127, 144–145)

Darlene Priscilla (p. 8)

Professional Bowlers Association (pp. 74, 79, 103, 142)

Professional Women's Bowling Association (pp. 47, 99, 116)

L. Todd Spencer (pp. 132, 149–151)

Wichita State University/Lisa Vint (p. 147)